the
student
cookbook

the
student
cookbook

great grub for the hungry and the broke

RYLAND PETERS & SMALL
LONDON • NEW YORK

Senior Designer Toni Kay
Senior Editor Céline Hughes
Picture Research Emily Westlake
Production Controller Toby Marshall
Art Director Leslie Harrington
Publishing Director Alison Starling

Indexer Sandra Shotter

First published in 2009.
This revised edition published in 2017
by Ryland Peters & Small, Inc.
341 East 116th Street
New York NY 10029

www.rylandpeters.com

10 9 8 7 6 5

Text © Nadia Arumugam, Susannah Blake,
Tamsin Burnett-Hall, Maxine Clark, Linda Collister, Ross
Dobson, Liz Franklin, Tonia George, Brian Glover, Nicola
Graimes, Rachael Anne Hill, Jennifer Joyce, Caroline Marson,
Jane Noraika, Louise Pickford, Jennie Shapter, Fiona Smith,
Sunil Vijayakar, Fran Warde, Laura Washburn, Lindy
Wildsmith, and Ryland Peters & Small 2009, 2017

Design and photographs © Ryland Peters & Small 2009, 2017

ISBN: 978-1-84975-868-0

Printed and bound in China

A CIP record for this book is available from
the Library of Congress.

Notes:
• All spoon measurements are level, unless
otherwise specified.

• Ovens should be preheated to the specified
temperature. Recipes in this book were tested using
a regular oven. If using a convection oven, follow
the manufacturer's instructions for adjusting
temperatures.

• All eggs are medium, unless otherwise specified.
Recipes containing raw or partially cooked egg,
or raw fish or shellfish, should not be served to the
very young, very old, anyone with a compromised
immune system, or pregnant women.

contents

Now that you're a fully fledged student and embracing independence, you're going to want to know how to cook up a storm in the kitchen. *The Student Cookbook* is here to allay any fears you might have about making your own dinner, and if you're already a budding cook, to give you some fresh inspiration. All the recipes are easy and delicious! Some are super-quick, while others need time in the oven or on the stove to work their magic. Either way, they are stress-free and designed to satisfy, whether you're coming home late with a mammoth hunger after a big night out, or you're having friends over for a lazy Sunday lunch. Make sure you check out the tips in the following pages before you get started— they will make life a whole lot easier and ensure that your culinary efforts are always successful, undaunting, and above all, fun.

introduction

kitchen know-how

The recipes in this book need the minimum of kitchen equipment. Some recipes, like the desserts, will require extras, e.g. a handheld electric whisk (which can be bought very cheaply), a baking pan for brownies, etc. but you can go a long way with these essentials:

2 or 3 sharp knives, including a serrated knife

wooden spoon

fish/egg slice

potato masher

garlic crusher

pepper mill

can opener

vegetable peeler

cheese grater

2 cutting boards (1 for meat and 1 for veg)

large mixing bowl

strainer

colander

1 large and 1 medium saucepan

skillet with a lid

baking sheet

roasting pan

ovenproof dish

measuring jug

weighing scales

a selection of airtight containers

kettle

toaster

aluminum foil

plastic wrap

parchment paper

paper towels

cleaning products, including washing up liquid, sponges, and surface cleaner

kitchen towels

oven gloves

Every recipe has at least two of these symbols:

 serves 4 This tells you roughly how many people the recipe should serve

 Q This is an extra-quick recipe, and shouldn't take you longer than 20 minutes once you've prepared the ingredients.

 V This is suitable for vegetarians, but that's not to say that meat-eaters won't enjoy it too!

 M This recipe includes some meat or poultry.

 F This recipe includes some fish or seafood.

Additionally, where a recipe calls for salt and black pepper, use sea salt and freshly ground black pepper if at all possible. They give the best flavor.

Whenever a recipe calls for olive oil, if you are using it raw (e.g. in a salad dressing or drizzled over vegetables), the extra virgin variety is the tastiest. For frying or roasting, use a basic (not extra virgin), mild variety.

handy ingredients

sea salt

black peppercorns

olive oil

vegetable or safflower oil

balsamic vinegar

red or white wine vinegar

dark or light soy sauce

tomato ketchup (as if you needed reminding!)

mustard

mayonnaise

long grain rice

risotto rice

dried pasta, including spaghetti

couscous

stock cubes or bouillon powder

canned chopped tomatoes

a selection of canned beans, such as cannellini, kidney

canned tuna

all-purpose flour

sugar

tomato paste

a selection of dried herbs, such as oregano

a selection of dried spices, such as curry powder, ground cumin, paprika, chili powder, or hot red pepper flakes

peanut butter

honey

butter or margarine

milk

onions

garlic

food safety

• Always keep your kitchen clean! Keep it tidy and disinfect worktops after use with a mild detergent or an antibacterial cleaner. Keep pets off surfaces and, as far as possible, keep them out of the kitchen.

• Store food safely to avoid cross-contamination. Keep food in clean, dry, airtight containers, always store raw and cooked foods separately, and wash utensils (and your hands) between preparing raw and cooked foods. Never put cooked food on a surface that you have used to prepare raw meat, fish, or poultry without thoroughly washing and drying the surface first.

• Wash your hands with hot, soapy water before and after handling food, and after you have handled raw meat and fish.

• Never put hot food into a refrigerator, as this will increase the internal temperature to an unsafe level. Cool leftover food quickly to room temperature, ideally by transferring it to a cold dish, then refrigerate. Cool large dishes such as stews by putting the dish in cold water. Stir occasionally (change the water often to keep the temperature low), then refrigerate once cool. During cooling, cover the food loosely with plastic wrap to protect it from contamination.

• Don't use perishable food beyond the "use-by" date as it could be a health risk. If you have any doubts about the food, discard it.

• Reheated food must be piping hot throughout before consumption. Never reheat any type of food more than once.

• Frozen meat and poultry should be thoroughly defrosted before you cook them otherwise the center may not be cooked, which could be dangerous.

• If you are going to freeze food, freeze food that is in prime condition, on the day of purchase, or as soon as a dish is made and cooled. Freeze it quickly and in small quantities, if possible. Label and date food and keep a good rotation of stock in the freezer.

• Always leave a gap in the container when freezing liquids, so that there is enough room for the liquid to expand as it freezes.

• Always let food cool before freezing it. Warm or hot food will increase the internal temperature of the freezer and may cause other foods to begin to defrost and spoil.

• Use proper oven gloves to remove hot dishes from the oven—don't just use a kitchen towel because you risk burning yourself. Kitchen towels are also a breeding ground for germs so only use them for drying, and wash them often.

- Hard cheeses such as Cheddar, Gruyère, and Parmesan will keep for up to 3 weeks if stored correctly. Once opened, fresh, soft cheeses such as cream cheese should be consumed within 3 days.
- Leftover canned foods should be transferred to an airtight container, kept in the refrigerator, and eaten within 2 days. Once cans are open, the contents should be treated as fresh food. This doesn't apply to food sold in tubs with resealable lids, such as cocoa powder.
- The natural oils in chiles may cause irritation to your skin and eyes. When preparing them, wear disposable gloves or pull a small polythene bag over each hand, secured with an elastic band around the wrist, to create a glove.
- If your kitchen is prone to over-heating, it is best to store eggs in their box in the refrigerator. Keep them pointed-end downward and away from strong-smelling foods, as they can absorb odors. Always use by the "best-before" date.
- Wash hands before and after handling eggs, and discard any cracked and/or dirty eggs.
- Cooked rice is a potential source of food poisoning. Cool leftovers quickly (ideally within an hour), then store in an airtight container in the refrigerator and use within 24 hours. Always reheat cooked cold rice until piping hot.

ingredients tips

- When substituting dried herbs for fresh, use roughly half the quantity the recipe calls for, as dried herbs have a more concentrated flavor.
- Chop leftover fresh herbs, spoon them into an ice-cube tray, top each portion with a little water, and freeze. Once solid, put the cubes in a freezer bag. Seal, label, and return to the freezer. Add the frozen herb cubes to soups, casseroles, and sauces as needed.
- The color of a fresh chile is no indication of how hot it will be. Generally speaking, the smaller and thinner the chile, the hotter it will be.
- To reduce the heat of a fresh chile, cut it in half lengthwise, then scrape out and discard the seeds and membranes (or core). See also "food safety" above for advice on handling chiles.
- Most vegetables keep best in the refrigerator, but a cool, dark place is also good if you lack fridge space. Potatoes should always be stored in the dark, otherwise they go green or sprout, making them inedible.
- To skin tomatoes, score a cross in the base of each one using a sharp knife. Put them in a heatproof bowl, cover with boiling water, leave for about 30 seconds, then transfer them to a bowl of cold water. When cool enough to handle, drain and peel off the skins with a knife.

- To clean leeks, trim them, then slit them lengthwise about a third of the way through. Open the leaves a little and wash away any dirt from between the layers under cold running water.
- Store flour in its original sealed packaging or in an airtight container in a cool, dry, airy place. Ideally, buy and store small quantities at a time, to help avoid infestation of psocids (very small, barely visible, gray-brown insects), which may appear even in the cleanest of homes. If you do find these small insects in your flour, dispose of it immediately and wash and dry the container thoroughly. Never mix new flour with old.
- If you run out of self-rising flour, mix 2 teaspoons baking powder with every 1¾ cups all-purpose flour. This will not be quite as effective but it is a good emergency substitute.
- Store raw meat and fish in the bottom of the refrigerator to prevent it dripping onto anything below.
- Store coffee (beans and ground) in the refrigerator or freezer, or it will go stale very quickly.
- Store oils, well sealed, in a cool, dark, dry place, away from direct sunlight. They can be kept chilled (though this is not necessary), but oils such as olive oil tend to solidify and go cloudy in the refrigerator. If this happens, bring the oil back to room temperature before use.

• To devein large shrimp, cut along the back of each shell using a sharp knife and lift or scrape out the dark vein. Alternatively, use a skewer to pierce the flesh at the head end of the shrimp, just below the vein, then use the skewer to gently remove the vein.

• Small pasta tubes and twists such as penne and fusilli are good for chunky vegetable sauces and some meat- and cream-based sauces. Larger tubes such as rigatoni are ideal for meat sauces. Smooth, creamy, butter-, or olive oil-based sauces and meat sauces are ideal for long strands such as spaghetti (so the sauce can cling to the pasta).

• Dried pasta has a long shelf life and should be stored in its unopened package or in an airtight container in a cool, dry place. Leftover cooked pasta should be kept in a sealed container chilled and used within 2 days. Ordinary cooked pasta does not freeze well on its own, but it freezes successfully in dishes such as lasagne and cannelloni. Allow 3–4 oz. dried pasta per person.

• Pasta must be cooked in a large volume of salted, boiling water. Keep the water at a rolling boil throughout cooking. Once you have added the pasta to the boiling water, give it a stir, then cover the pan to help the water return to a boil as quickly as possible. Remove the lid once the water has started boiling again (to prevent the water boiling over), and stir occasionally. Check the manufacturer's instructions for cooking times. When it is ready, cooked pasta should be al dente—tender but with a slight resistance.

• As an accompaniment, allow 2–3 oz. uncooked rice per person or for an entrée, up to 4 oz.

• Rice may be rinsed before cooking to remove tiny pieces of grit or excess starch. Most packaged rice is checked and clean, however, so rinsing it is unnecessary and will wash away nutrients. Risotto rice is not washed before use, but basmati rice usually is—rinse it under cold water until the water runs clear.

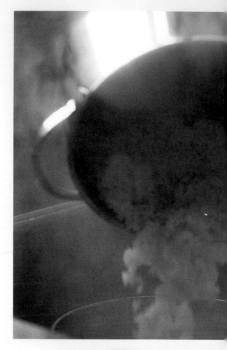

taste tips

• Try mixing a pinch or two of ground spices such as curry powder, chili powder, or turmeric with bread crumbs or flour, and use to coat foods before frying. Add ground spices such as cinnamon, mixed spice, or ginger to fruit crumble toppings. A pinch or two of ground nutmeg will perk up mashed potatoes, cheese sauce, cooked spinach, and rice puddings.

• Stir whole-grain mustard into mashed potatoes or mayonnaise before serving to add extra flavor. Mustard also enhances salad dressings and sauces. A pinch or two of English mustard powder added to cheese dishes will enhance the flavor.

• If you add too much salt to a soup or casserole, add one or two peeled and cubed potatoes to soak up the salt, cooking until tender. Discard the potatoes before serving.

• An excellent way of thickening soups is to stir in a little oatmeal. It adds flavor and richness too. A small amount of instant mashed potato stirred in at the last minute is also a good way of thickening soup.

• Add a little pearl barley to soups and stews—it will add flavor and texture and have a thickening effect.

• A teaspoon or two of pesto sauce stirred into each portion of a hot vegetable soup just before serving will liven it up.

• For a tasty and creamy salad dressing, mash some blue cheese and stir it into mayonnaise, or a mixture of mayonnaise and plain Greek yogurt.

• Add some health and a satisfying crunch to salads by tossing in a handful or two of lightly toasted seeds or chopped nuts just before serving. Good ideas include sunflower, sesame, or pumpkin seeds and hazelnuts, walnuts, pecans, or pistachios. Toasted seeds can also be sprinkled over cooked vegetables.

• If you overcook an omelet, let it cool and use it as a sandwich filling. Chop the omelet and combine it with mayonnaise and snipped chives, if you like.

• Bulk out a pasta or rice salad by adding a can of drained and rinsed beans such as chickpeas, red kidney beans, or black-eye beans.

• For an extra-crunchy crumble topping, replace 1 oz. of the flour with the same weight of chopped nuts, rolled oats, or oatmeal, or replace granulated sugar with brown sugar.

kitchen wisdom

• To remove odors from a container that you want to use again, fill the container with hot water, then stir in 1 tablespoon baking powder. Let it stand overnight, then wash, rinse well, and dry before use.

• If you transfer foods from their original packaging to your own storage containers, stick the food label onto the container so you can easily identify its contents and you have a record of the manufacturer's cooking instructions, if necessary. Make a note of the "best-before" or "use-by" date on the container, too.

• For convenient single servings, freeze portions of homemade soup in large, thick paper cups or small individual containers. Remove them from the freezer as required, defrost, and reheat the soup thoroughly before serving.

• To make salad dressings or vinaigrettes, put all the ingredients in a clean jar, seal, and shake well. Alternatively, put the ingredients straight into the salad bowl and whisk together well before adding the salad.

• Liquors with an alcohol content of 35% or over can be kept in the freezer—this is ideal for those which should be served ice-cold.

• To remove fishy odors after preparing fish, rub the cut surface of a lemon over your hands, the knife, and cutting board. Rubbing your hands with vinegar or salt, then rinsing and washing them, will also help to get rid of unpleasant fishy smells.

microwave safety

• The more food you are cooking, and the colder it is, the longer it will take to cook in a microwave.

• When microwaving items such as sausages or bacon that may spit during cooking, cover them loosely with a paper towel, to avoid too much splattering.

• Many foods need to be covered during microwaving. Use either microwave-safe plastic wrap, a plate, or a lid. Pierce the plastic wrap, or leave a gap at one side if using a plate or lid, to allow excess steam to escape.

• Never operate a microwave when it is empty, as the microwaves will bounce back to and damage the oven components.

• Be careful when stirring heated liquids in a container in the microwave, as they can bubble up without warning.

• After food has been removed from the microwave, it will continue to cook due to the residual heat within the food, so adhere to standing times when they are given in recipes.

• Use a microwave with a built-in turntable if possible, and make sure that you turn or stir the food several

times during cooking to ensure even cooking throughout. The food towards the outer edges usually cooks first.

• Metal containers, china with a metal trim, foil, or crystal glass (which contains lead) should not be used in a microwave. Metal reflects microwaves and may damage the oven components. Microwave-safe plastic containers, ovenproof glass, and ceramic dishes are all suitable, as is most household glazed china. Paper plates and paper towels can be used to reheat food for short periods. Roasting bags (pierced) may be used in a microwave.

snacks and sides

guacamole

Guacamole is so easy to make and very versatile. Scoop it up with the Tortilla Chips below, use it as a dip for sticks of raw veg, spread it on toast, or have it with the Beef Fajitas on page 183 or the Chile Chicken Enchiladas on page 78.

Using a small, sharp knife, cut the avocado in half all around from top to bottom. Twist the fruit gently and pull the two halves away from each other. Using a teaspoon, scoop out the flesh from each half into a small bowl, and throw away the seed and the skin. Gently mash the flesh with a fork to make a lumpy purée.

Stir in the diced tomato, 2 teaspoons of the lime juice, and the garlic. Season with salt and pepper. Mix all the ingredients together with the fork—the mixture should be a bit lumpy. Taste and add more lime juice or salt and pepper as needed. Eat immediately before it turns brown.

serves
2–4

Q

V

1 large, very ripe avocado

1 large or 2 small tomatoes, diced

juice of 1 lime

1 small garlic clove, crushed

a big pinch of salt

a big pinch of black pepper

home-baked *tortilla* chips

Turn ready-made soft wheat tortillas into a crunchy snack by baking them in the oven.

Preheat the oven to 325°F.

Using kitchen scissors, cut each tortilla into 8 wedges. Spread the wedges in one layer, not overlapping, on the baking sheet.

Bake them in the preheated oven for 15 minutes until they turn crisp and dry. Eat while still warm or let cool first.

serves
4–6

Q

V

4 large or 6 medium wheat flour tortillas

a large baking sheet

tzatziki

Greek tzatziki is a versatile, low-fat dip and it also makes a great salad dressing or accompaniment to grilled chicken and fish or roast Mediterranean-style vegetables.

½ a cucumber, seeded and grated

2 teaspoons salt

1 garlic clove, crushed (optional)

⅔ cup Greek yogurt

juice of ½ a lemon

Mix the grated cucumber and salt together and leave for 10 minutes. Put the cucumber in the center of a clean kitchen towel, gather up the edges, and twist to squeeze as much moisture out as possible. Put the cucumber in a bowl with the remaining ingredients and stir to combine. The tzatziki will keep in the refrigerator for 3 days.

Variations:

Beet tzatziki Add 1 medium raw or 2 bottled beets, grated, and 2 tablespoons snipped chives to the mixture. This makes a great accompaniment to boiled new potatoes.

Olive tzatziki Stir ⅓–½ cup finely chopped pitted black or green olives into the yogurt and cucumber mixture.

garlic and tomato naan

This recipe calls for puffy naan bread. If none is available, you can use an Italian ciabatta loaf. Slice it in half through the middle and spread the butter over the cut sides.

2 tomatoes

3 tablespoons butter, softened

2 garlic cloves, crushed

2 tablespoons dried oregano

2 x 4-oz. naan breads

salt and black pepper

Preheat the oven to 400°F.

Peel the tomatoes using the instructions on page 10. Seed the tomatoes, remove the cores, and finely chop the flesh. Let cool.

Put the softened butter, garlic, and oregano in a bowl and mix well. Add the chopped tomatoes and mix well to combine. Spread each naan bread with half of the mixture. Season with salt and pepper.

Bake in the preheated oven for 10–15 minutes until hot. Cut into slices and serve immediately.

tzatziki

cheese on toast

2 thick slices of white bread

4 oz. cheese, such as Brie, Cheddar, or a soft creamy goat cheese

a few drops of Worcestershire sauce (optional)

pickles, relish, or chutney, to serve

This is one of those dishes that's perfect when you get back late from a night out—quick, delicious, and washing-up-free. It tastes great with almost any chutney or relish. Two slices just won't be enough!

Preheat the broiler.

Toast the bread under the broiler on one side only. Slice, grate, or spread your chosen cheese onto the untoasted side of the bread. Add a few splashes of Worcestershire sauce, if using, and broil for 2–3 minutes until melted and bubbling.

Serve with pickles, relish, or chutney and tuck in.

cinnamon toast

2 thick slices of white bread

unsalted butter, for spreading

1¼ tablespoons sugar

½ teaspoon ground cinnamon

The quickest treat yet invented—hot buttered toast sprinkled with cinnamon-flavored sugar, then broiled until crunchy. Thick slices of bread, challah, or brioche (two kinds of soft bread) work best, but you can also use bagels or English muffins split in half.

Preheat the broiler.

Toast the 2 slices of bread in a toaster, then spread with butter.

Mix the sugar with the cinnamon, then sprinkle it over the buttered toast to cover in an even layer.

Put the toast under the broiler for 30 seconds to 1 minute until the sugar has melted and looks bubbly, then carefully remove it.

Let cool for a minute (the sugar is very hot and will burn your lips) before eating.

tomato, basil, and
mozzarella toasts

cheese
on toast

tomato, basil, and mozzarella toasts

These irresistible, juicy toasts make a perfect snack or small bite to serve with drinks. They're great just with tomatoes and basil, but even better with a chunk of mozzarella on top.

makes **12**

V

Put the tomatoes and basil in a bowl. Spoon over the olive oil, season well with salt and pepper, and toss lightly. Set aside for about 15 minutes.

Preheat the broiler.

Toast the ciabatta slices on both sides under the broiler until crisp and golden. Rub the cut side of the garlic on each piece of toast, then spoon the tomato and basil mixture on top. Add a piece of mozzarella to each one, spoon over the juices remaining in the bowl, and sprinkle with extra oil, if using. Grind a little more pepper on top and serve.

8 oz. cherry tomatoes, halved

1–1½ handfuls of fresh basil leaves, roughly torn

3 tablespoons olive oil, plus extra for drizzling (optional)

12 slices of ciabatta, about 1 inch thick

1 garlic clove, halved

6 oz. mozzarella, torn into bite-size pieces

salt and black pepper

giant prosciutto, brie, and tomato toasts

giant *prosciutto*, *brie*, and *tomato* toasts

This mammoth, melting toast is the closest thing to an instant pizza that you could wish for—with the juicy tomatoes and arugula adding a wonderful fresh zing.

serves 2 · Q · M

10–12 cherry tomatoes

1 teaspoon balsamic vinegar

1 tablespoon olive oil

1 ciabatta loaf, halved horizontally

4 slices of prosciutto or thinly sliced smoked ham

6 oz. Brie

2 handfuls of arugula

black pepper

Cut the tomatoes in half and put in a bowl. Sprinkle with the vinegar and olive oil, season with pepper, and toss gently. Set aside.

Preheat the broiler.

Set the ciabatta under the broiler, cut side down. Toast until crisp and golden. Meanwhile, cut each slice of prosciutto into 3 pieces.

Turn the bread over and arrange the strips of prosciutto and slices of Brie on the uncooked side. Broil for a further 5 minutes or so until the bread is golden, the ham crisp, and the cheese golden and bubbling.

Spoon the tomatoes on top, top each toast with a handful of arugula, and serve immediately.

mushrooms on toast

Another treat that's good at any time of day, these fragrant mushrooms are really rich and garlicky. Pile them up on thick slices of hot buttered whole-wheat toast or a crusty roll.

serves 2 · Q · V

1 tablespoon olive oil

2 shallots, finely sliced

1 garlic clove, crushed

6 oz. button mushrooms

¼ cup white wine

1 sprig of fresh thyme

2 thick slices of whole-wheat bread

butter, for spreading

salt and black pepper

Heat the oil in a pan, add the shallots, and fry gently for 2 minutes, then add the garlic and cook for a further minute.

Add the mushrooms, toss to coat in the garlicky oil, then add the white wine, thyme, and a pinch of salt. Increase the heat and bring to a boil, then let bubble gently for about 10 minutes until the mushrooms are tender and the juices have been absorbed.

When the mushrooms are nearly cooked, toast the bread on both sides and spread with butter. Season the mushrooms with pepper, check if they need any more salt, then pile onto the toast.

spicy fried *potatoes* and *chorizo* on toast

3 tablespoons olive oil

6 oz. new potatoes, boiled and cut into bite-size chunks

4 oz. raw chorizo sausage, cut into bite-size chunks

1 garlic clove, crushed

½ teaspoon hot red pepper flakes

4 slices of country-style sourdough bread

salt and black pepper

This manly feast is not for the faint-hearted and is perfect when you need something quick, tasty, and really filling. The crisp, golden potatoes absorb the flavors of the chorizo, and the rich, spicy, garlicky oil is just delicious when it soaks into the toast. Sprinkle with a little more red pepper flakes for extra heat.

Heat the oil in a large skillet until hot, then add the potatoes and fry for about 5 minutes. Add the chorizo and continue frying, turning occasionally, until the potatoes are crisp and golden. Sprinkle with the garlic and red pepper flakes and fry for a further 2 minutes.

Meanwhile, toast the bread in a toaster. Spoon the potato and chorizo mixture on top, drizzling over any extra oil from the skillet, then serve.

pesto and *mozzarella* toastie

1 ciabatta roll, halved horizontally

1–2 teaspoons pesto

4 thin slices of mozzarella

black pepper

A variation on classic cheese on toast but with an Italian twist. This is a particularly good choice if piles of melted cheese puts that diet at risk: mozzarella is lower in fat than Cheddar.

Preheat the broiler.

Lightly toast the uncut side of each half of the ciabatta roll under the broiler.

Turn the ciabatta halves over and spread with the pesto. Top with the mozzarella and return it to the broiler. Broil for about 3 minutes until the mozzarella melts and begins to color. Sprinkle with a little black pepper before serving.

spicy fried potatoes
and chorizo on toast

*leeks and tomatoes
on toast*

leeks and *tomatoes* on toast

This is a really tasty suggestion for a quick breakfast, lunch, or dinner. Much more than just tomatoes on toast...

Heat the oil in a skillet, add the leeks and mushrooms, and cook over medium heat for 4–5 minutes, or until tender.

Meanwhile, toast the bread, then spread with butter.

Add the tomatoes and herbs to the leek mixture and cook for a further 1–2 minutes, or until heated through. Season with pepper. Serve the toast topped with the tomato and leek mixture.

Variation This would make an ideal filling for warmed split pita. Add 1 thinly sliced and seeded red or yellow bell pepper at the same time as the leeks, if you like. If you can buy some wild mushrooms, use them instead of the button ones for extra flavor.

serves **2** | Q | V

1 teaspoon olive oil

2 small leeks, thinly sliced

10 button mushrooms, about 2 oz., sliced

4 slices of whole-wheat bread

butter, for spreading

7 oz. cherry tomatoes, halved

3 teaspoons finely chopped fresh basil leaves

2 teaspoons finely chopped fresh oregano

2 teaspoons finely chopped fresh flatleaf parsley

black pepper

sardines and *tomato* on toast

Canned sardines are an ideal pantry standby, and are a great source of calcium, vitamin D, and long-chain omega-3 fatty acids—great brain food!

Toast the bread in a toaster, then lightly spread with mayonnaise.

Put the sardines on top of the toast, then mash slightly with a fork. Arrange the chopped tomato on top, then squeeze over a little lemon juice. Season with black pepper before serving.

serves **1** | Q | F

1 slice of whole-wheat bread

mayonnaise, for spreading

2 oz. canned boneless, skinless sardines in olive oil, drained

1 small tomato, halved, seeded, and roughly chopped

a squeeze of lemon juice

black pepper

little fried *mozzarella* and *tomato* sandwiches

6½ oz. mozzarella, torn into bite-size pieces

16 small, thin slices of bread

3–4 tomatoes, thinly sliced

3 eggs

3 tablespoons olive oil, to fry

salt and black pepper

serves 4

V

These are lovely because they are crisp and eggy on the outside and gooey and creamy on the inside. They are a popular snack all over Italy. Add slices of ham if you like.

Dot the mozzarella over 8 of the bread slices and lay the slices of tomato over the top. Top with the remaining bread slices and press lightly to seal.

Crack the eggs into a bowl, then beat with a fork until they are smooth. Pour them into a shallow container in which you can fit the sandwiches. Lay the sandwiches in the egg and leave them for 2–3 minutes to soak up the egg. Turn them over and leave them for another 2–3 minutes so that the other side is soaked in egg too.

Heat a little of the olive oil in a nonstick skillet and fry the sandwiches on one side for about 3 minutes, until the bread is golden. Carefully turn the sandwiches over and fry for a further 2–3 minutes, until that side is golden too; the cheese inside should be well melted.

Cut the sandwiches in half diagonally and serve them straightaway.

garlic and *parsley* bread

2 garlic cloves, crushed

a handful of fresh flatleaf parsley, chopped

¼ teaspoon hot red pepper flakes

olive oil

1 ciabatta loaf, split horizontally

salt and black pepper

serves 4

Q

V

Everyone loves this easy bread—similar to garlic bread but with a little kick from hot red pepper flakes. Eat it by itself or alongside a stew to mop up the juices left in your plate.

Preheat the broiler.

Sprinkle the garlic, parsley, red pepper flakes, salt, and pepper evenly over the opened bread halves. Drizzle generously with olive oil, then cook under the broiler until golden. Cut the bread into chunks and serve with a big bowl of pasta, such as Rigatoni with Bacon and Beans on page 73.

*little fried mozzarella
and tomato samdwiches*

gruyère, sharp cheddar,
and scallion panini

french toast and fried tomatoes

Who says French toast is just for breakfast? Topping it with fried tomatoes makes a juicy, tasty snack. Frying tomatoes seems to intensify their flavor and the heat makes them soft and velvety—truly delicious on eggy bread.

serves
4

Q

V

4 eggs

¼ cup milk

4 slices of bread

4 tablespoons butter

4 ripe tomatoes, halved

salt and black pepper

Beat together the eggs and milk in a large, shallow dish and add some salt and pepper. Add the bread and let soak for 5 minutes on each side so that all the egg mixture is absorbed.

Heat a large, nonstick skillet over medium heat. Add the soaked bread and cook over medium-low heat for 3–4 minutes on each side.

In a separate skillet or pan, melt the butter. Add the tomatoes and fry on each side for 2 minutes, then serve on top of the hot French toast.

gruyère, sharp cheddar, and *scallion* panini

This is no ordinary grilled cheese sandwich. It works best with a panini grill but you can use a sandwich toaster instead. The mixture of strong cheeses with scallion is pure heaven.

makes
2

Q

V

4 slices of sourdough bread

2 oz. Gruyère, grated

2 oz. sharp Cheddar, grated

2 scallions, thinly sliced

salt and black pepper

vegetable oil, for brushing

Preheat a panini grill or sandwich toaster. Lay the slices of bread out. Divide the cheeses between the two sandwiches, add the scallions, and season with salt and pepper. Put the tops on. Brush both sides of the panini with a little oil and toast in the preheated panini grill for 2–3 minutes, or according to the manufacturer's instructions. The bread should be golden brown and the filling warmed through.

Note Try this panini with a dollop of grainy mustard on the side for dipping and a baby spinach salad.

6 oz. canned tuna, drained

3–3½ tablespoons mayonnaise

½ tablespoon capers, rinsed
and finely chopped

2 gherkins or 1 dill pickle
in sweet vinegar, diced
fairly finely

¼ red bell pepper, diced finely

1 tablespoon chopped fresh
tarragon (optional)

2 large, thick slices of white
crusty bread

4 large, thin slices Swiss
cheese, such as Gruyère
or Emmenthal

black pepper

tuna melt

serves
2

Q

F

This is the ultimate tuna melt. Use any kind of white bread—crusty rustic sourdough or a simple sandwich loaf—just make sure the slices are large and thick.

Put the tuna in a bowl and flake the flesh. Add the mayonnaise, capers, gherkins, bell peppers, and tarragon (if using) and mix. Season with pepper.

Preheat the broiler.

Toast the bread on one side under the broiler, then turn it over and spread the tuna thickly on the uncooked side. Put 2 cheese slices on top of each toast and broil for about 5 minutes until the cheese is golden and bubbling.

Note Look for tuna canned in water rather than brine as the capers are salty enough already.

olive oil, for brushing

2 large soft wheat flour
tortillas

3½ oz. canned tuna, drained
and mashed with a fork

6 slices of mozzarella,
about 2¼ oz. total weight

10 fresh basil leaves

black pepper

mozzarella and *tuna* quesadilla

serves
2–4

Q

F

This golden, satisfying tortilla parcel is filled with melted mozzarella and tuna. Diced sweet bell pepper, chopped scallions, or herbs, such as chives can also be added, if liked.

Lightly brush a large nonstick skillet with oil. Put one tortilla into the skillet so it fits snugly. Spoon the tuna over the tortilla, leaving a 1-inch gap around the edge. Top the tuna with the mozzarella and basil, then season with pepper to taste.

Put the second tortilla on top of the filling, pressing it down around the edges. Put the skillet over medium-low heat and cook the quesadilla for 3 minutes until the tortilla is golden and beginning to crisp.

To cook the other side of the quesadilla, put a large plate on top of the skillet and carefully flip it over to release the quesadilla onto the plate, then slide it back into the skillet. Cook the tortilla for another 3 minutes until golden and the mozzarella is melted. Slice into 6 wedges and serve.

bacon, potato, and red leicester panini, with tabasco sauce

mozzarella and tuna quesadilla

bacon, potato, and *red leicester* panini, with tabasco sauce

Save your leftover baked or roasted potatoes to create this fiery, filling panini—not for the faint-hearted!

Preheat a panini grill or a sandwich toaster. Cut the top and bottom off the ciabatta so that it is about 1 inch thick. Save the crusts for another use. Slice open lengthwise and then cut in half.

Add a little oil to a skillet and fry the bacon until crisp. Remove from the skillet and drain on paper towels. Keep the skillet hot, add the potato slices, and season with salt and pepper. Fry on both sides until crisp around the edges. Divide the bacon and potatoes between the two sandwiches. Add a dash of Tabasco and top with the cheese. Brush both sides of the panini with a little oil and toast in the preheated panini grill for 3 minutes, or according to the manufacturer's instructions. The bread should be golden brown and the filling warmed through.

makes
2

Q

M

1 ciabatta loaf

6 slices of smoked bacon

1 large cooked potato, sliced

2 oz. Red Leicester or Monterey Jack, thinly sliced

2 teaspoons Tabasco sauce

salt and black pepper

vegetable oil, for frying and brushing

*spicy
vegetable wrap*

spicy vegetable wrap

serves **4**

Q

V

The heat in this wrap comes from harissa, a red chile paste from Morocco. If you are not that keen on very spicy food, simply leave it out or replace it with humous.

Spread the tortillas sparingly with a little harissa, if using, leaving a 1-inch border around the edge. Sprinkle with a layer of grated carrot, then layers of zucchini, scallions, tomatoes, and lettuce.

Roll the tortilla up tightly into a cigar shape. Cut in half across the middle and eat immediately or wrap in plastic wrap until you are ready.

4 soft wheat flour tortillas

harissa (optional)

2 carrots, grated

1 zucchini, grated

2 scallions, finely chopped

½ cup half-baked tomatoes

8 iceberg lettuce leaves, chopped

scrambled eggs

serves **2–3**

Q

V

There are two ways of cooking scrambled eggs: in the microwave or on the stovetop in a nonstick pan. The second method is better because the eggs become creamy and delicious.

Whisk the eggs together with the milk and add salt and pepper. Melt the butter in a medium nonstick pan, then add the egg mixture, stirring frequently until it reaches a creamy consistency. Serve with a sprinkling of chopped chives and hot buttered toast.

6 eggs

4 tablespoons milk

2 tablespoons butter

salt and black pepper

chopped chives, to serve

hot buttered toast

scrambled eggs

baked *brunch* omelet

This is a great way to cook an omelet—once prepared, it can finish cooking in the oven, so you can get on with something else. Make sure the skillet handle is ovenproof or removable.

Preheat the oven to 400°F.

Heat the oil in the skillet, add the bacon, onion, and potato, and fry for 6 minutes, or until the potatoes start to brown. Add the mushrooms and fry for 2 minutes.

Meanwhile put the eggs and milk in a large bowl and whisk briefly with a fork, just enough to mix the yolks and whites. Season with salt and plenty of pepper. Stir in three-quarters of the Cheddar.

Using a slotted spoon, transfer the potato mixture to the bowl of eggs and mix well. Add the butter to the skillet and, when it starts to foam, pour in the omelet mixture. Sprinkle with the remaining cheese and transfer to the preheated oven. Cook for 12–15 minutes, or until just set. Loosen the edges with a spatula and slide onto a serving plate.

 serves **2–3**

 M

2 tablespoons safflower oil

4 slices of smoked bacon, cut into strips

1 onion, finely sliced

1 potato, cubed

1½ cups sliced button mushrooms

5 extra-large eggs

scant ½ cup milk

¾ cup grated sharp Cheddar

1 tablespoon butter

salt and black pepper

an 8-inch skillet (measure the base, not the top)

farmhouse sauté with *bacon* and *onions*

A great late-night feast for a gang of friends. You'll need some leftover cooked potatoes.

Heat the olive oil in a large skillet over medium heat. Add the sliced cooked potatoes and fry on each side until golden. Remove the potatoes with a slotted spoon and set aside to drain on paper towels.

Add the onion, bacon, and thyme to the skillet and cook, stirring constantly, until the mixture is crisp and golden. Add the cooked potatoes and salt and pepper to taste. Mix well and serve at once.

 serves **4**

 Q

 M

3 tablespoons olive oil

2 lbs. cooked potatoes, thickly sliced

2 onions, diced

8 oz. bacon, chopped

3 sprigs of fresh thyme

salt and black pepper

sausage and bacon rolls

16 thin slices of
streaky bacon

a little mustard

8 sausages

olive oil, for brushing

4 warm buttered soft rolls
or even small naan bread
or pita

tomato ketchup, to serve

serves
4

Q

M

There's nothing quite like a warm sausage-filled roll. Dotting
the sausages with mustard and wrapping them in bacon just
adds to the taste experience and the cooking smells will waken
even the most hungover. Get these under way while you make
a big pot of tea or coffee.

Preheat the broiler.

Spread a little mustard over each slice of bacon. Wrap 2 slices around each
sausage. Put the sausages on the rack of a broiler pan so that the loose ends
of the bacon are underneath the sausage. Brush with a little oil and broil for
about 6–8 minutes on each side, depending on the thickness of the sausage,
until the bacon is crisp and the sausage cooked through. Serve in buttered
rolls with plenty of ketchup.

cheat's mini pizzas

4 English muffins

⅔ cup tomato purée

toppings of your choice, such
as diced ham, pineapple, corn
kernels, flaked tuna, sliced
mushrooms, bell peppers, and
shredded fresh herbs, etc.

½ cup grated mozzarella
or Cheddar

serves
4

Q

These ultra-quick pizzas are the answer to fast food when faced
with mates so hungry they simply can't wait for the real thing.
Tomato purée can be used as an instant tomato sauce, but if you
have canned chopped tomatoes or even jarred tomato sauce left
over from last night's pasta, that will do too. Top the pizzas
with anything you like!

Preheat the oven to 400°F.

Slice the muffins in half horizontally. Spread the tomato purée over them,
then top with a topping of your choice, or simply with a little grated cheese.

Bake in the preheated oven for 8–10 minutes until the muffins are crispy
round the edges and the cheese is golden and bubbling.

sausage and bacon rolls

baked *sweet potatoes* with *lentils* and *bacon*

2 medium sweet potatoes

½ cup red split lentils

1 cup hot vegetable stock

1 garlic clove, crushed

½ onion, very finely chopped

1 celery stalk,
very thinly sliced

½ tablespoon soy sauce

1 tablespoon tomato paste

3 slices of bacon, broiled
and chopped

⅓ cup grated sharp Cheddar

an ovenproof dish

serves
2

M

Sweet potatoes and lentils are low-glycemic index foods, which means they release their sugars into the blood stream at a slow and steady rate, helping to keep your energy levels constant. So although this is essentially a cheesy baked potato, it's much healthier, and it will keep you going for longer. For maximum ease, top the sweet potato with canned baked beans instead.

Preheat the oven to 400°F.

Lightly prick the sweet potatoes with a fork and bake directly on the shelves of the preheated oven for 35–40 minutes until soft when gently squeezed. Remove and leave until cool enough to handle.

Meanwhile, put the lentils in a saucepan, add the stock, and bring to a boil. Cover, reduce the heat, and simmer for 20–25 minutes until soft. Add more stock or water if the lentils start to dry out.

Meanwhile, put the garlic, onion, celery, soy sauce, and 3–4 tablespoons water in a nonstick skillet and heat gently for about 10 minutes or until the vegetables are soft. Add them to the saucepan of cooked lentils along with the tomato paste, chopped broiled bacon, and half the grated cheese. Mix well, then reheat gently, stirring occasionally, until hot.

Turn off the oven and preheat the broiler.

Cut the cooked sweet potatoes in half. Put them in the ovenproof dish and top with the lentil mixture. Sprinkle with the remaining cheese and cook under the broiler for 10 minutes or until the cheese is golden and bubbling.

Note To cook the sweet potatoes in a microwave, wrap them in paper towels and cook each one individually on HIGH for 4–4½ minutes. Leave for 1 minute before topping with the lentils and broiling as in the recipe above.

potato wedges with *garlic* and *paprika*

Potatoes any way are great, but there's something particularly appealing about wedges. These have a delicious spice mix coating. Take a bowl of mayonnaise and stir in a bit of crushed garlic for dunking the wedges. Hard to imagine anything better.

serves
4

V

3 lbs. potatoes, unpeeled but well scrubbed

1 dried bay leaf (optional)

⅛ cup olive oil

3 garlic cloves, crushed

1 tablespoon dried oregano

1 teaspoon paprika

salt and black pepper

If the potatoes are large, cut in half lengthwise, otherwise leave whole. Put in a large saucepan of water with the bay leaf (if using). When the water boils, add a heaped tablespoon of salt and cook until just tender, but not completely soft. Drain and let cool slightly.

When the potatoes are cool enough to handle, cut into wedges. Put in a large dish and add the oil, garlic, oregano, paprika, and salt and mix well.

Preheat the oven to 450°F.

Arrange the wedges in a single layer on a baking sheet and bake in the preheated oven until browned, 30–40 minutes. Sprinkle with pepper.

baked sweet potatoes with lentils and bacon

potato wedges with garlic and paprika

*sesame sweet
potato wedges*

sesame *sweet potato* wedges

This nutty dipping sauce works brilliantly with the sweetness of the potatoes. Serve them with with very cold beer when friends come round for an evening in front of the TV.

serves
6–8

V

Preheat the oven to 400°F.

Arrange the sweet potato wedges in a single layer on the baking sheet, then sprinkle with the olive and sesame oils, sesame seeds, and salt. Roast in the preheated oven for 35 minutes or until tender (the cooking time will vary depending on the size of the wedges).

Meanwhile, to prepare the dipping sauce, put the peanut butter, lime juice, chile, soy sauce, and tomato ketchup in a bowl with 4 tablespoons hot water and stir until smooth. Add salt and pepper to taste, then pour into a saucepan and heat gently.

Sprinkle the wedges with the cilantro and serve with a separate bowl of the dipping sauce.

Note To simplify this recipe even further, serve the wedges with storebought sweet chili sauce.

1½ lbs. sweet potatoes, well scrubbed but unpeeled, cut lengthwise into thick wedges

2 tablespoons olive oil

1 tablespoon toasted sesame oil

1 tablespoon sesame seeds

cilantro, coarsely torn or chopped, to serve

salt and black pepper

Dipping sauce

2 tablespoons peanut butter

1 tablespoon lime juice

½ red chile, seeded and very finely chopped

1 tablespoon soy sauce

1 tablespoon tomato ketchup

a baking sheet

creamy *mustard* mash

Mashed potato with mustard is true comfort food. For a change, try adding grated cheese, chopped herbs, and fried onions.

serves
4

V

Put the potatoes in a saucepan of water, bring to a boil, then lower the heat and simmer for 20 minutes or until tender. Drain the cooked potatoes thoroughly, then return them to the pan and set it over low heat. Shake the pan and let the potatoes steam dry.

Put the milk, olive oil, and butter in a separate saucepan and warm gently.

Mash the potatoes well, being sure to crush out all the lumps.

Add the warm milk mixture, mustard, salt, and pepper to the mashed potatoes. Using a wooden spoon, beat well until smooth and well blended. Taste and season with salt and pepper as necessary.

1½ lbs. potatoes, cut into large cubes

⅔ cup milk

3 tablespoons olive oil

4 tablespoons butter

1 tablespoon English mustard powder

salt and black pepper

rosemary potatoes

serves
4

2¼ lbs. floury potatoes (such as Yukon Gold), peeled and cut into small chunks

¼ cup olive oil

2 garlic cloves, crushed

a small handful of fresh rosemary needles, chopped

salt and black pepper

a roasting pan

Potatoes roasted with rosemary and garlic are heavenly. They are the perfect accompaniment to a Sunday lunch.

Preheat the oven to 400°F.

Put the potatoes in a bowl, cover with water, and let them soak for 10 minutes, then drain and pat dry with paper towels.

Pour the olive oil into the roasting pan and put it in the preheated oven. Heat for 3–4 minutes until the oil is hot.

Remove the pan from the oven, add the potatoes, and return the pan to the oven. Roast the potatoes for about 35 minutes, until crisp and golden and almost soft.

Remove the pan from the oven and scatter the garlic, rosemary, and some salt and black pepper over the potatoes. Stir and return to the oven for 5–10 minutes longer. Drain the potatoes on paper towels before serving.

bubble and squeak patties

makes
6

1 cup shredded Savoy cabbage

1½ cups mashed potatoes

¼ cup grated sharp Cheddar

1½ teaspoons Dijon mustard

1 small egg, lightly beaten

flour, for dusting

2 tablespoons safflower or canola oil

salt and black pepper

This is a great way of using up leftover mashed potatoes. Serve the patties with broiled tomatoes and chicken or vegetarian sausages. They're also good cold as a snack.

Steam or boil the cabbage for 2–3 minutes until just tender. Let cool, then squeeze out any excess water using your hands.

Finely chop the cabbage, then put it in a bowl with the mashed potatoes, cheese, and Dijon mustard. Season to taste and mix until combined, then stir in the egg. Divide the mixture into 6. Using floured hands, form each portion into a patty shape. Lightly dust each patty with flour.

Pour the oil into a large nonstick skillet and heat. Cook 3 patties at a time for 3–4 minutes each side until golden, adding a little more oil if necessary. Keep the cakes that you've cooked warm while you cook the rest. Drain the patties on paper towels to remove any excess oil before serving.

rosemary potatoes

*potato skins
with green dip*

potato skins with green dip

This recipe makes a lot of potato skins but they are so delicious that you'll be glad you made this many.

Preheat the oven to 350°F.

Using a sharp knife, pierce each potato right through the middle. Bake in the preheated oven for about 1 hour 10 minutes or until cooked through. Remove and set aside until cool enough to handle. Raise the heat to 425°F. Cut each potato in half lengthwise and scoop out the potato middles, leaving a thin layer lining the skin. Cut each skin into 4 wedges. Brush oil over the potato skins and arrange in a single layer on the prepared baking sheet. Bake at the top of the oven for 30 minutes, moving the potatoes around occasionally to ensure even cooking. Remove from the oven and reduce the heat to 400°F. Sprinkle with cheese and return to the oven for 5–10 minutes until the cheese is melted.

To make the dip, put the sour cream, chives, scallions, and parsley into a bowl. Add salt and pepper to taste and mix well.

makes 24

V

3 large baking potatoes

3 tablespoons olive oil

1 cup grated sharp Cheddar

Green dip

½ cup sour cream

a handful of fresh chives, snipped

3 scallions, chopped

a bunch of fresh flatleaf parsley, chopped

salt and black pepper

a baking sheet, lightly greased

three-cheese *cauliflower*

How can you improve on this classic comfort food? Use a variety of high-end cheeses to make it even richer.

Preheat the oven to 375°F.

Plunge the cauliflower florets into a saucepan of boiling water. Bring back to a boil, then simmer for 4 minutes and drain well.

Put the cheeses in a bowl, sprinkle in the cornstarch, and mix to coat the cheese evenly. Transfer to a nonstick saucepan, add ¾ cup water, and gently bring to a slight simmer, stirring constantly until you have a smooth sauce.

Put the cauliflower in the ovenproof dish and pour the cheese sauce all over it. Bake in the preheated oven for 15 minutes, until golden on top. Take care when serving as the cheese gets extremely hot.

serves 4

V

1 cauliflower, cut into florets

3½ oz. Gruyère, grated

3½ oz. Emmenthal, grated

3½ oz. Beaufort or other hard, strong cheese, grated

1 teaspoon cornstarch

salt and black pepper

a shallow ovenproof dish, about 8 x 10 inches

broccoli cheese

1 lb. broccoli, cut into florets

¼ cup safflower oil

¼ cup flour

1¾ cups milk

¾ cup grated sharp Cheddar, plus extra for sprinkling

an ovenproof dish

serves
4

V

A little like the Three-cheese Cauliflower on page 49, only with a lot less cheese for a lighter conscience.

Preheat the broiler.

Steam the broccoli over gently simmering water for 8 minutes or until it is tender but still has some bite. Drain and transfer to the ovenproof dish.

Heat the oil in a small saucepan and stir in the flour. Cook, stirring, for 2 minutes. Remove the pan from the heat and gradually stir in the milk. Return the pan to the heat and cook, stirring continuously, until the sauce thickens. Add the grated cheese and stir until melted. Pour the sauce over the broccoli and sprinkle with a little more grated cheese. Cook under the broiler for 10–15 minutes until the cheese is golden brown and bubbling.

stir-fried *sesame cabbage*

2 tablespoons peanut oil

1 tablespoon toasted sesame oil

2 garlic cloves, sliced

1 red chile, seeded and sliced

2 lbs. Savoy cabbage, finely shredded

1 tablespoon chopped cilantro

juice of ½ a lemon

½ cup dry-roasted peanuts

2 tablespoons sesame seeds, lightly toasted in a dry skillet

salt and black pepper

serves
4

Q

V

Soggy old boiled cabbage—no way, this quick stir-fried dish is crunchy, spicy, and lemony and makes an ideal accompaniment to pork dishes, or as a quick veggie snack by itself.

Heat the two oils together in a wok or large, deep skillet, add the garlic and chile, and stir-fry over high heat for 30 seconds.

Add the cabbage and stir-fry for a further 2–3 minutes until golden and the cabbage is starting to soften.

Add the cilantro, lemon juice, peanuts, sesame seeds, salt, and pepper, stir well, and transfer to a warmed dish. Serve at once.

broccoli
cheese

*rice noodle salad
with shrimp*

cannellini beans
with *garlic* and *parsley*

These make such an easy and delicious side dish. If you like, you could leave them without heating and serve them as a small salad or pick-me-up before heading out for the evening.

Put the beans in a saucepan and add the onion, garlic, olive oil, and half the parsley. Season with salt and pepper and stir gently but thoroughly. Set aside for about 30 minutes to allow the flavors to develop.

Heat the beans gently until warm. Stir in the remaining parsley and drizzle with a little extra olive oil.

serves
6

V

2 x 14-oz. cans cannellini beans, drained and rinsed

1 small onion, finely chopped

2 garlic cloves, crushed

⅓ cup olive oil, plus extra to serve

4 tablespoons fresh parsley leaves, finely chopped

salt and black pepper

rice *noodle* salad with *shrimp*

This is a delicious and sustaining lunch that is quick to make. If you'd like to spice it up a little more, add some chopped scallions, cilantro, and red chile.

Cook the noodles according to the package instructions. Drain, toss them in a little of the oil, and let cool in the colander for 10 minutes.

Heat the remaining oil in a wok or large skillet and add the ginger, garlic, shrimp, beans, and carrot. Cook over medium heat for 4 minutes, stirring constantly. Add the mixture to the cooled noodles and mix well. Sprinkle with cashew nuts and toasted sesame seeds.

serves
6

Q

F

5 oz. thin rice noodles

2 tablespoons vegetable oil

½ inch fresh ginger, peeled and finely chopped

1 garlic clove, crushed

6 oz. cooked peeled shrimp

2 oz. fine green beans, trimmed

1 carrot, cut into matchsticks

juice of ½ a lime

¼ cup chopped cashew nuts

1 tablespoon sesame seeds, lightly toasted in a dry skillet

3½ oz. dried pasta,
such as penne

1 red onion, thinly sliced

3 celery stalks, chopped

1 carrot, grated

¼ cup raisins

3-inch piece of cucumber,
chopped

¼ cup cooked corn kernels

14-oz. can tuna, drained
and flaked

⅛ cup mayonnaise

⅛ cup Greek yogurt

salad greens

8 oz. cherry tomatoes, halved

tuna pasta salad

This is a good idea for a hurried lunch, but it's also ideal for
making in advance and putting in a container for lunch later on.

Cook the pasta in a large saucepan of boiling water for 12–15 minutes, or
according to the manufacturer's instructions, until al dente. Drain, refresh
under cold running water, and transfer to a large bowl.

Cut the onion slices in half to form half moons, then add to the bowl along
with the celery, carrot, raisins, cucumber, corn, and tuna.

Mix the mayonnaise with the yogurt and add it to the salad. Stir gently until
well coated. (You can make the recipe up to this point and store, covered, in
the refrigerator for up to 2 days.)

To serve, line a plate with salad greens, put a serving of the pasta salad
on top, and scatter over a few halved tomatoes.

1 cup shredded white
cabbage

1 cup shredded red cabbage

1¼ cups grated carrots

½ onion, thinly sliced

2 teaspoons sugar

1 tablespoon white wine
vinegar

¼ cup mayonnaise

¼ cup sour cream

salt and black pepper

sour cream coleslaw

You could use plain light, rather than sour cream if you like
here but the sharp flavor of sour cream works particularly well.

Put the white and red cabbage, carrots, and onion in a colander and
sprinkle with the salt, sugar, and vinegar. Stir well and let drain over
a bowl for 20 minutes.

Transfer the vegetables to a clean kitchen towel and squeeze out any excess
liquid. Put them in a large bowl and stir in the mayonnaise and cream.
Season to taste with salt and pepper and serve.

greek country salad

greek country salad

Choose very ripe tomatoes that are still firm but full of flavor. Splash out on beefsteak tomatoes, or those on the vine, if you can, as they will be more flavorful.

Cut the tomatoes into wedges. Put them in a large bowl along with the lettuce, cucumber, olives, and feta, if using.

Put all the dressing ingredients in a bowl, whisk well with a fork, then drizzle over the salad and toss well to coat evenly. Sprinkle with the oregano and serve at once.

serves **4**

Q

V

4 tomatoes

1 romaine lettuce heart, sliced

2 small cucumbers, sliced

1¾ cups pitted black olives

8 oz. feta, crumbled (optional)

1 teaspoon dried oregano

Dressing

¼ cup olive oil

¼ cup red wine vinegar

½ teaspoon sugar

salt and black pepper

easy entrées

scotch broth

scotch *broth*

Barley is traditionally used in Scotch broth, but here we have brown rice in its place. And it goes without saying that soy sauce is never used in traditional Scottish fare but it works well with the other flavors in this recipe. This broth is dead simple, with a minimum of ingredients, but you could add some herbs if you like. Thyme, in particular, likes being with lamb.

serves
4

M

Heat the oil in a large saucepan. Add the carrot, leek, celery stalks, and leaves and cook over high heat for 5 minutes, stirring often. Add the lamb, stock, soy sauce, rice, and 1 quart water and bring to a boil.

Reduce the heat to low, cover with a tight-fitting lid, and let the soup simmer for 1 hour. Season to taste with salt and pepper and serve with soft, buttered rolls on the side.

2 tablespoons olive oil

1 carrot, diced

1 leek, diced

2 celery stalks, diced and leaves chopped

1 lb. stewing lamb, well trimmed of fat and cubed

2 cups chicken stock

1 tablespoon light soy sauce

½ cup brown rice

salt and black pepper

4 soft dinner rolls, buttered, to serve

soup with *pasta shells, peas, artichokes,* and *chile*

An incredibly speedy soup that has a wonderful, fresh flavor, yet is made almost entirely from pantry ingredients. Enjoy a taste of summer all year round.

serves
4

Q

M

Heat the oil in a large saucepan, add the onion, garlic, chiles, and bacon and cook for 4–5 minutes until golden.

Add the oregano, artichokes, and peas and stir-fry for 2 minutes. Add the stock, bring to a boil, then simmer for 10 minutes.

Meanwhile, bring another large saucepan of water to a boil. Add a good pinch of salt, then the pasta, and cook until al dente, or according to the manufacturer's instructions.

Drain the pasta and add it to the soup. Pour into bowls, sprinkle with Parmesan, then serve.

1 tablespoon olive oil

1 onion, finely chopped

2 garlic cloves, crushed

2 red chiles, thinly sliced

4 slices of smoked bacon, finely chopped

1 teaspoon dried oregano

14-oz. can artichoke hearts in water, drained and quartered

¾ cup frozen peas

5 cups hot chicken or vegetable stock

⅔ cup any dried pasta shapes

salt and black pepper

2 tablespoons grated Parmesan, to serve

chunky *chickpea* soup

2 tablespoons olive oil

1 leek, thinly sliced

1 small fennel bulb, diced

3½ oz. pancetta, diced

1 carrot, grated

1 potato, diced

6 cups hot chicken or vegetable stock

14-oz. can chickpeas, rinsed and drained

3 oz. fresh spinach, chopped

½ cup grated Parmesan

salt and black pepper

serves 4

M

This version of minestrone is a meal in its own right. Packed with winter vegetables, it's a "one-pot wonder" that improves with age. Pancetta is available ready chopped and pre-packed.

Heat the oil in a saucepan. Add the leek, fennel, and pancetta and cook for 5 minutes over high heat, until the leek softens and the pancetta really flavors the oil. Add the carrot, potato, stock, and chickpeas and bring to a boil. Reduce the heat and simmer for 20 minutes. Season to taste with salt and pepper, then add the spinach. Cook over low heat for 5 minutes, until the spinach has wilted throughout the soup.

Serve with Parmesan sprinkled over the top.

Variation Add 3½ oz. small pasta (try the little rice-shaped pastas such as risoni or orzo) instead of chickpeas and simmer until the pasta is cooked through before adding the final few ingredients. This will give you a very thick soup that you may even need a fork to eat!

vegetable, ham, and *barley* broth

1 tablespoon safflower oil

2 onions, sliced

⅔ cup pearl barley, rinsed

1 celery stalk, sliced

5 cups hot chicken or vegetable stock

2 dried bay leaves

a sprig of fresh thyme

2 large carrots, halved lengthwise and sliced

1 sweet potato, peeled and cut into bite-size chunks

7 oz. thickly cut cooked ham, diced, or ⅔ cup canned chickpeas, drained and rinsed

salt and black pepper

serves 4

M

This nurturing broth makes a nutritious light lunch, dinner, or between-meal snack. It is filling enough to be served on its own, but if you are feeling really peckish, you could have it with a slice of bread and a chunk of cheese.

Heat the oil in a large saucepan and sauté the onions, half-covered, for 5 minutes. Add the barley and stir so that it is coated in the oil. Cook for another 2 minutes, stirring continuously.

Add the celery, stock, bay leaves, and thyme to the pan. Bring to a boil, then reduce the heat and simmer, half-covered, for 30 minutes, occasionally skimming away with a large spoon any froth from the barley that rises to the surface.

Add the carrots, sweet potato, and ham and cook for another 15–20 minutes until the vegetables and barley are tender. Season with salt and pepper to taste, then remove the bay leaves and thyme before serving.

chunky
chickpea
soup

chickpea, tomato,
and chorizo soup

chickpea, tomato, and chorizo soup

This soup tastes fantastic and is refreshingly simple to prepare. Make sure you buy the correct chorizo—you want the short, fat cured sausages. They are ready to eat but are much better fried.

serves **4**

M

6 oz. cured chorizo, roughly chopped

1 red onion, chopped

2 garlic cloves, crushed

14-oz. can chopped tomatoes

2 fresh thyme sprigs

14-oz. can chickpeas, drained and rinsed

4 cups hot vegetable stock

salt and black pepper

Put the chorizo in a large saucepan over medium heat and cook until it starts to release its oil. Continue to cook, stirring, for 4–5 minutes until it is lovely and crisp. Add the red onion and garlic and turn the heat right down to allow them to soften in the chorizo's paprika-infused oil. After 6–7 minutes the onion and garlic should be translucent and glossy. Add the tomatoes and thyme and turn the heat back up. Cook for 5 minutes to intensify the flavor, then add the chickpeas and stock. Return to a boil, cover, and simmer for 15 minutes.

Remove the thyme. Season well with salt and pepper and simmer for a further 10 minutes to allow all the flavors to get to know one another. Transfer to bowls and serve.

split pea and sausage soup

The thick wintry mix of tender lentils with chunks of sausage in this soup is so filling, it's almost a casserole—perfect to get you ready for a long walk, or just a long snooze on the couch.

serves **6**

M

2 tablespoons olive oil

1 onion, chopped

1 leek, chopped

2 celery stalks, chopped

a pinch of grated nutmeg

1½ cups yellow split peas

6 cups hot chicken stock

2 dried bay leaves

8 oz. sausages

salt and black pepper

Heat the olive oil in a large saucepan and cook the onion, leek, and celery gently over low heat for 8–10 minutes. Add the nutmeg and stir in. Add the split peas and mix into the vegetables. Add the stock and bay leaves, cover, and simmer for 45 minutes or until the peas are tender and beginning to get mushy when pressed with the back of a spoon.

Meanwhile, preheat the broiler.

Broil the sausages until cooked, then roughly chop. Add to the soup and cook for a further 10 minutes. Season with salt and pepper and serve.

3 tablespoons butter

5 oz. pancetta or smoked bacon, cubed

1 onion, sliced

2 carrots, finely chopped

10 oz. new potatoes (unpeeled), thinly sliced

2 tablespoons flour

2½ cups milk

1⅘ cups hot chicken or vegetable stock

3 dried bay leaves

2½ cups corn kernels (defrosted if frozen)

3 tablespoons heavy cream

salt and black pepper

corn and *pancetta* chowder

serves 4

M

Although there are many variations, a chowder is often a creamy stock thickened with potatoes and spiked with the rich flavor of smoky bacon. This one is bowl food of the most warming and comforting kind. Roaring fire optional.

Heat the butter in a large saucepan and fry the pancetta until crisp. Add the onion, carrots, and potatoes, cover, and cook gently for 15–20 minutes until soft. Stir occasionally.

Sprinkle the flour into the pan and cook for 1 minute, stirring it into the vegetables. Pour in the milk gradually, blending it with the flour, then add the stock and bay leaves; bring to a gentle simmer. Add the corn and cook for 5 minutes.

Remove from the heat, stir in the cream, and season with salt. Pour into bowls and serve with a fresh grinding of pepper

6 cups warm chicken stock

½ cup long grain rice

14 oz. cooked chicken, shredded

3 eggs

juice of 1 lemon

croutons, to serve

chicken avgolemono

serves 4

Q

M

Use up any chicken you might have left over after a hearty Sunday roast, or buy some pre-cooked chicken from the supermarket. Either way, this soup requires minimum effort.

Heat the stock in a large saucepan and add the rice. Bring to a boil and simmer for 15 minutes or until the rice is tender. Add the chicken and warm through for 2–3 minutes.

In the meantime, whisk the eggs and lemon juice in a small bowl. Add a ladleful of the warm stock and whisk until thinned. Remove the soup from the heat and gradually pour in the egg mixture, whisking to amalgamate it. It should thicken in the residual heat, but if you need to, place it over low heat for just 3–4 minutes, stirring the bottom of the pan to thicken. Do not return to high heat once the egg has been added, or it will scramble.

Pour the soup into bowls and garnish with croutons.

corn and pancetta
chowder

spaghetti bolognese

Like many classic, handed-down recipes, there are countless versions of Bolognese sauce. This one uses ground beef and prosciutto, as well as dried porcini mushrooms, which may seem extravagant but try it and see—it's worth the extra little ingredients to make it taste this good. It benefits from being chilled overnight, so it tastes even better the second time round.

⅛ cup dried porcini mushrooms, rinsed

1 tablespoon olive oil

1 onion, finely chopped

1¼ lbs. ground beef

⅔ cup coarsely chopped prosciutto

⅓ cup Marsala or sherry

3 cups canned crushed tomatoes

10 oz. dried pasta, such as spaghetti or linguine

salt and black pepper

Parmesan shavings, to serve

Put the porcini into a bowl, cover with boiling water, and set aside for 20 minutes until softened.

Heat the oil in a large saucepan, add the onion, and cook for 2 minutes. Add the ground beef and prosciutto and cook for 3–4 minutes, stirring, until evenly browned.

Drain the porcini and discard the water. Chop the porcini, then add to the pan with the Marsala and canned tomatoes. Cover and simmer for 1 hour, stirring occasionally, until rich and dark. Add salt and pepper to taste.

Meanwhile, bring a large saucepan of water to a boil. Add a good pinch of salt, then the pasta, and cook until al dente, or according to the manufacturer's instructions.

Drain the pasta and transfer to plates or bowls. Top with the Bolognese sauce and Parmesan shavings, then serve.

2 tablespoons olive oil

1 onion, finely chopped

2 garlic cloves, crushed

4 anchovy fillets in oil,
drained and chopped

2 red chiles, finely chopped

4 ripe tomatoes, chopped

1 tablespoon salted capers,
rinsed well and chopped

⅓ cup red wine

12 oz. dried pasta, such as
penne or rigatoni

¾ cup small pitted black
olives

2 tablespoons chopped fresh
flatleaf parsley

black pepper

grated Parmesan, to serve

pasta with *puttanesca sauce*

serves
4

F

Puttanesca sauce is chile-hot, with a salty depth from anchovies
and capers. More importantly, it's a great excuse to crack open
a bottle of red wine, a little of which you need in this recipe.

Heat the oil in a saucepan, then add the onion, garlic, anchovies, and
chiles. Cook over medium heat for 4–5 minutes until softened and golden.
Add the tomatoes and cook for 3–4 minutes, stirring occasionally, until
softened. Add the capers, wine, and pepper to taste, then cover and
simmer for 20 minutes.

Meanwhile, bring a large saucepan of water to a boil. Add a good pinch
of salt, then the pasta, and cook until al dente, or according to the
manufacturer's instructions.

Drain well and return the pasta to the warm pan. Add the tomato sauce,
olives, and parsley and toss to mix. Transfer to bowls and serve topped
with grated Parmesan.

6 oz. dried pasta,
such as spaghetti

⅓ cup olive oil

4 garlic cloves, halved

6 anchovy fillets
in oil, drained

salt and black pepper

white *spaghetti*

serves
2

Q

F

This is one of those dishes that saves your life when you get
home tired and hungry. Always keep some anchovies, olive oil,
and spaghetti in the cupboard to make this at short notice.

Bring a large saucepan of water to a boil. Add a good pinch of salt,
then the pasta, and cook until al dente, or according to the manufacturer's
instructions.

Put the olive oil and garlic in a small saucepan and heat very gently over
low heat for 4–5 minutes until the garlic is pale golden but not browned.
Remove and discard the garlic. Add the anchovies and ⅓ cup water to the
pan and simmer rapidly, whisking with the fork until the anchovies have
almost dissolved into the mixture. Add plenty of pepper and a tiny pinch
of salt. Drain the pasta and return it to the warm pan. Add the anchovy
mixture and toss well to mix. Transfer to bowls and serve.

*pasta with
puttanesca sauce*

*fusilli with
sausage ragu*

*tuscan tuna
and bean pasta*

13 oz.–1 lb. dried pasta,
such as fusilli

1½ lbs. raw chorizo sausage

2 tablespoons olive oil

1 onion, finely chopped

2 garlic cloves, crushed

2 tablespoons chopped
fresh sage

2 x 14-oz. cans chopped
tomatoes

⅓ cup red wine

2 tablespoons tomato paste

2 tablespoons chopped fresh
flatleaf parsley

salt and black pepper

fusilli with *sausage ragu*

serves
4–6

Chorizo, the spicy Spanish sausage, is used in this rich ragu,
but you could substitute any Italian-style sausage if you prefer.

M

Bring a large saucepan of water to a boil. Add a good pinch of salt,
then the pasta, and cook until al dente, or according to the manufacturer's
instructions.

Cut away the skins of the sausages and finely chop the sausage meat.

Heat the olive oil in a saucepan and gently fry the onion, garlic, sage, and
salt and pepper over low heat for 10 minutes, or until soft and lightly golden.
Add the sausage meat and stir-fry over medium heat for 5 minutes, or until
browned. Add the canned tomatoes, wine, and tomato paste, bring to a
boil, cover, and simmer gently for 1 hour, or until the sauce has thickened.
Season with salt and pepper to taste, stir in the parsley, and serve.

tuscan *tuna* and *bean* pasta

This is the fastest, easiest pasta sauce you can make and it's so filling it can be served as a meal in itself with some crusty bread. Make the whole amount, even if it's just for yourself, then refrigerate the rest in an airtight container for tomorrow, or freeze it for another time.

Bring a large saucepan of water to a boil. Add a good pinch of salt, then the pasta, and cook until al dente, or according to the manufacturer's instructions.

Meanwhile, put the tomatoes, tuna, beans, stock, cilantro, and salt and pepper in a saucepan and heat, stirring occasionally, for about 5 minutes until piping hot. Spoon the sauce over the pasta, stir, and serve.

Note If you have a food processor or stick blender, you can purée the ingredients together first before heating them up in a saucepan.

serves **6**

Q

F

1 lb. dried pasta, such as penne

14-oz. can chopped tomatoes

6½ oz. canned tuna, drained

10 oz. canned beans, such as red kidney, butter bean, or navy, drained and rinsed

⅓ cup hot vegetable stock

1 tablespoon chopped cilantro

salt and black pepper

cherry tomato puttanesca sauce

Here's another version of the Puttanesca Sauce from page 68. This one is made using cherry tomatoes to add extra texture and a slightly sweeter flavor.

Heat the olive oil in a large skillet and gently fry the garlic, red pepper flakes, and seasoning for 3–4 minutes, or until softened. Add the tomatoes, stir-fry for 1 minute, then stir in the olives, anchovies, capers, lemon juice, and basil and heat through. Serve topped with grated cheese, if desired.

serves **4**

¼ cup olive oil

2 garlic cloves, crushed

a pinch of hot red pepper flakes

1 lb. cherry tomatoes, halved

3½ oz. pitted black olives, halved

6 anchovy fillets in oil, drained and chopped

¼ cup capers in brine, drained and washed

juice of 1 lemon

2 tablespoons chopped fresh basil

salt and black pepper

grated cheese, to serve

rigatoni with *bacon* and *beans*

Rustic and hearty, this pasta dish makes a warming dinner. Canned beans are a convenient pantry standby, plus nutritionists say that three heaping tablespoons of beans count as a single portion of the recommended "five-a-day" so you can dish up a generous helping knowing that you're doing good!

serves
2

M

1 tablespoon olive oil

1 onion, chopped

1 garlic clove, crushed

1 teaspoon dried oregano

4½ oz. smoked bacon, roughly chopped

1⅜ cups canned crushed tomatoes

a pinch of sugar

1 teaspoon tomato paste

3½ oz. canned borlotti beans, drained and rinsed

6 oz. dried pasta, such as rigatoni or penne

salt and black pepper

Heat the oil in a saucepan and fry the onion for 8 minutes until softened, then stir in the garlic, oregano, and bacon and cook for another 2 minutes.

Pour in the canned tomatoes and stir in the sugar and tomato paste. Bring to a boil, then reduce the heat to low and simmer, half-covered, for 10 minutes, stirring occasionally. Add the beans, stir, and cook for another 5 minutes.

Meanwhile, cook the pasta in plenty of boiling salted water, following the manufacturer's instructions, until al dente. Drain, reserving 4 tablespoons of the cooking water. Set aside.

Add the cooked pasta and reserved cooking water to the sauce and heat through before serving. Season with salt and pepper to taste.

Note There is a temptation, when you're short on cash and time, to turn to pasta for sustenance a little too often. Although pasta is not bad for you, it's not especially nutritious, so it's best to eat it in moderation, or at least in as healthy a form as possible. The recipe above is a good option, but you can also make any of the other pasta recipes in this book kinder to your diet by using whole-wheat pasta and avoiding pairing it with unhealthy temptations, such as garlic bread.

7–10 oz. basmati rice

2 tablespoons vegetable oil

1 onion, grated

3 garlic cloves, crushed

2 inches fresh ginger, peeled and sliced

1 mild red chile, chopped

1 teaspoon ground turmeric

2 teaspoons curry powder

1 teaspoon ground coriander

1 teaspoon ground cumin

1 lb. cooked peeled shrimp

14-oz. can chopped tomatoes

juice of 2 limes

freshly chopped cilantro

2½ tablespoons vegetable oil

1 small onion, finely chopped

2 garlic cloves, crushed

2 tablespoons chili sauce

2 teaspoons shrimp paste

1 large skinless chicken breast fillet, about 8 oz., diced

6¼ oz. uncooked peeled shrimp, roughly chopped

3¼ oz. carrot, finely grated

6¼ oz. canned corn kernels

3¼ oz. green beans, trimmed and finely chopped

1 lb. cold, cooked basmati rice

1 tablespoon light soy sauce

2 extra-large eggs, lightly beaten with a pinch of salt

shrimp curry

 serves 4

 Q

F

Tiger or jumbo peeled shrimp are ideal for this colorful, citrus-flavored curry.

Cook the rice according to the manufacturer's instructions.

Meanwhile, heat the oil in a large pan, add the onion, garlic, ginger, and chile, and cook for 5 minutes over medium heat. Add the turmeric, curry powder, ground coriander, and cumin and mix well. Add the shrimp and cook for 3 minutes. Pour in the tomatoes and lime juice, season with salt and pepper, and bring to a boil. Reduce the heat and simmer for 5 minutes. Garnish with freshly chopped cilantro and serve with the cooked rice.

Variation: For a vegetarian option, replace the shrimp with 8 oz. halved button mushrooms and 8 oz. frozen peas (see photograph on front cover).

indonesian fried rice

 serves 4

 Q

 M

 F

This beats takeout egg fried rice hands down. And the great thing is you can use yesterday's leftover boiled rice. Remember to make sure the rice is piping hot when you serve it as it can be dangerous to eat partially reheated cooked rice.

Heat 2 tablespoons of the oil in a large skillet until hot. Add the onion and stir-fry over high heat for 2–3 minutes, or until softened and golden. Add the garlic and continue to cook for 1 minute. Add the chili sauce and shrimp paste and cook for 1 minute, then throw in the chicken. Stir-fry for 2 minutes, then add the shrimp and cook until opaque and cooked through.

Throw in the carrot, corn, and green beans and cook for 2 minutes, or until the beans are cooked but still crunchy. Add the rice and soy sauce to the wok and mix through. Cook until the rice is piping hot, then remove from the heat and set aside.

Heat the remaining oil in a large skillet and pour in the beaten eggs. Let set into a thin omelet. Transfer to a cutting board and let cool for 1 minute. Roll up the omelet tightly and slice as thinly as possible. Transfer the fried rice to bowls and garnish with the omelet.

shrimp curry

*thai green
chicken curry*

thai green *chicken* curry

There is a wonderful fragrance to Thai curries, and they make a fantastic shared meal. Build up the chile content gradually until you find a spiciness that everyone enjoys.

Heat the oil in a large saucepan, add the onion, ginger, garlic, lemon grass, and chile and cook over low heat for 5 minutes. Add the chicken and cook for a further 5 minutes.

Add the kaffir lime leaves and curry paste and mix well. Slowly pour the coconut milk into the curry, mixing constantly. Pour in ⅓ cup water along with the lime juice, bring to a simmer, and cook gently for 5 minutes. Add the broccoli and beans and simmer for another 3 minutes. A large bowl of plain boiled jasmine rice is a good accompaniment.

serves **4**

M

2 tablespoons vegetable oil

1 onion, sliced

2 inches fresh ginger, peeled and sliced

2 garlic cloves, crushed

1 lemon grass stem, chopped

1 mild green chile, diced

4 skinless chicken breast fillets, sliced

2 kaffir lime leaves

2 tablespoons Thai green curry paste

¾ cup coconut milk

juice of 1 lime

½ cup broccoli florets

½ cup green beans, trimmed

salt and black pepper

indian *lamb* curry

This is a simple but unbeatable curry that needs plenty of time on the stove-top to produce meltingly soft lamb.

Heat half the oil in a large pan, add the onion, ginger, chile, and garlic, and cook over high heat for 1 minute, stirring constantly. Add the spices, then continue to cook for 1 minute. Transfer to a plate.

Heat the remaining tablespoon of oil in the pan and fry the lamb briskly until browned, about 5 minutes. Return the onion mixture to the pan and add the tomatoes. Season and pour in just enough water to cover. Bring to a boil, then lower the heat, cover, and simmer for 1½–2 hours, stirring occasionally. The lamb should be tender and the sauce thick.

Just before serving, add the cilantro. Plain boiled basmati rice is a good accompaniment, as is plain yogurt to temper the heat of the curry.

serves **4–6**

M

2 tablespoons vegetable oil

1 onion, sliced

2 inches fresh ginger, peeled and chopped

1 mild red chile, chopped

3 garlic cloves, crushed

1 teaspoon garam masala

1 teaspoon mild curry powder

2 lbs. lamb stewing meat, cut into 1-inch pieces

14-oz. can chopped tomatoes

a bunch of cilantro, chopped

salt and black pepper

chile chicken enchiladas

serves
4–6

M

3 tablespoons safflower oil

1 lb. skinless chicken breast fillets, cut into strips

1 large onion, chopped

1 red chile, seeded and finely chopped

1 garlic clove, crushed

2 tablespoons tomato paste

14-oz. can chopped tomatoes

14-oz. can pinto beans, rinsed and drained

1 tablespoon chopped cilantro

8 corn tortillas, warmed

⅔ cup sour cream

2¼ oz. sharp Cheddar, grated

salt and black pepper

shredded scallions, to sprinkle

an ovenproof dish, lightly greased

Corn tortillas, pinto beans, and chiles are synonymous with Mexican cooking. This recipe combines chicken with a fiery tomato sauce as a filling for the soft tortillas, which are topped with sour cream and Cheddar before baking. It makes a perfect lunch or supper dish served with a crisp leaf salad.

Preheat the oven to 375°F.

Heat 2 tablespoons of the oil in a large nonstick skillet, add the chicken, and stir-fry for 4–5 minutes, or until golden. Remove with a slotted spoon, put into a bowl, and set aside.

Add the remaining oil to the skillet, then the onion and fry for 5 minutes. Add the chile and garlic and fry for 1–2 minutes more, or until the onions are soft and golden. Stir in the tomato paste, canned tomatoes, and ⅓ cup cold water. Cook for 2–3 minutes and season with salt and pepper.

Add just under half the sauce to the chicken with the beans and cilantro and mix together. Spoon 2 heaping tablespoons of the chicken mixture onto the middle of each warmed tortilla and roll up to enclose the filling. Place seam-side down in the prepared ovenproof dish and top with the remaining tomato sauce.

Spoon the sour cream along the center of the tortillas and sprinkle with the grated cheese. Bake in the preheated oven for 15–20 minutes or until golden and bubbling. Sprinkle over the scallions and serve.

*chicken lemon
skewers*

chicken lemon skewers

If you can, cook these skewers on an outdoor grill—the yogurt becomes delicious and slightly crunchy. Failing that, they are delicious under the broiler, indoors on a cloudy day, to give you a taste of sunshine. Note that they need to marinate overnight in the refrigerator before cooking.

serves 4

M

1 lb. skinless chicken breast fillets

Marinade

1 cup plain yogurt

2 tablespoons olive oil

2 garlic cloves, crushed

grated zest and juice of 1 unwaxed lemon

1–2 teaspoons ground chiles

1 tablespoon chopped cilantro

salt and black pepper

12 bamboo skewers, soaked in cold water for 30 minutes

Cut the chicken fillets lengthwise into ⅛-inch thick strips and put into a shallow ceramic dish. Put all the marinade ingredients into a bowl, stir well, and pour over the chicken, turn to coat, cover, and marinate in the refrigerator overnight.

The next day, preheat an outdoor grill or broiler.

Thread the chicken onto the soaked bamboo skewers, zig-zagging the meat back and forth as you go. Cook on the grill or under the broiler for 3–4 minutes on each side until charred and tender. Let cool slightly before serving.

super-easy *lamb* skewers

Dinner doesn't get much easier than this, but served with Rosemary Potatoes from page 46 and a simple side of fresh chopped tomatoes, you have a lovely Italian-style meal for four with minimum effort. The lamb is best done on a grill pan.

serves 4

1 lb. lamb fillet, cut into bite-size chunks

salt

tomato salad, to serve

Rosemary Potatoes (page 46), to serve (optional)

12 bamboo skewers, soaked in cold water for 30 minutes

a ridged grill pan

Push the pieces of lamb onto the skewers until you run out of lamb (leave 2 inches clear at each end of the skewers). Season the lamb with salt.

Heat the grill pan until quite hot. Lay the skewers on the pan and cook for about 10 minutes, until the lamb is cooked through and dark brown. Turn them over once halfway through cooking. You will need to cook them in batches.

Serve with a tomato salad and some Rosemary Potatoes, if liked.

1 tablespoon olive oil

1 tablespoon lemon juice

12 small dried bay leaves

1 small unwaxed lemon, halved and cut into 12 small wedges

10 oz. skinless turkey breast fillets, cut into 12 large bite-size chunks

salt and black pepper

Potato, olive, and tomato salad

14 oz. new potatoes, scrubbed

12 pitted black olives, quartered

2 vine-ripened tomatoes, seeded and cut into chunks

3 tablespoons chopped fresh flatleaf parsley

a handful of fresh basil leaves

1½ tablespoons lemon juice

1½ tablespoons olive oil

4 bamboo skewers, soaked in cold water for 30 minutes

turkey and *bay* skewers with potato, olive, and tomato salad

serves
2

M

Turkey makes a nice alternative to chicken. It's cheap, easy to cook, and very low in fat so it is a healthy choice, too. These turkey kabobs are infused with the tangy flavor of lemon and bay leaves.

To make the potato, olive, and tomato salad, cook the potatoes in boiling water for 12 minutes, or until tender. Drain and let cool slightly. Halve or quarter the potatoes if large, then put in a salad bowl with the olives, tomatoes, parsley, and basil leaves. Mix together the lemon juice and olive oil and pour over the salad. Season with salt and pepper to taste and toss until everything is combined.

Preheat the broiler and line a broiler pan with aluminum foil.

To make the kabobs, mix together the olive oil and lemon juice.

To assemble the skewers, follow this order of ingredients for each one: bay leaf, lemon, turkey, lemon, turkey, bay leaf, lemon, turkey, bay leaf.

Arrange the 4 skewers in the broiler pan. Brush with the olive oil and lemon juice mixture and broil for 4 minutes. Turn the skewers, brush with more of the olive oil and lemon juice, and broil for another 3–5 minutes, or until the turkey is cooked through.

Serve the turkey skewers with the potato, olive, and tomato salad.

pepperoni, bell pepper, and *crouton* frittata

A frittata is Italy's version of an open omelet and it is one of the most convenient ways to use up leftovers in the refrigerator. This one is packed with tasty roasted bell peppers and pepperoni, and must be served immediately, otherwise it goes on cooking and loses its soft creaminess. It can also be left to cool, cut into wedges, and enjoyed as part of a lunch-on-the-go the following day.

Break the eggs into a bowl and beat well using a fork. Season well with salt and pepper and add half the cheese and the scallion. Mix well.

Melt half the butter in the ovenproof skillet. Add the bread pieces and toss them for 2–3 minutes over high heat until golden brown and crispy. Remove from the heat and set aside.

Preheat the broiler.

Add the remaining butter and the garlic to the skillet, and when the butter starts to froth, add the beaten eggs. Turn the heat down and let the eggs cook gently for a few minutes. Arrange the pepperoni and bell peppers on the top and sprinkle with the remaining cheese and reserved croutons.

Put the skillet under the broiler and cook for a further 2–3 minutes until the frittata is puffed and just set but still wobbly. Remove from the broiler and serve immediately with a crisp green salad or a tomato and basil salad.

Variation Also delicious made with any combination of the following: crumbled firm goat cheese, sliced mushrooms, baby spinach leaves, zucchini, or sliced cooked potatoes.

serves
2

Q

M

4 eggs, lightly beaten

1 oz. grated Gruyère cheese

1 scallion, thinly sliced

2 tablespoons butter

1 oz. firm white bread, torn into small pieces

1 garlic clove, crushed

1 roasted bell pepper, cut into strips

1 oz. sliced pepperoni

salt and black pepper

a medium-size, ovenproof skillet

2 teaspoons coriander seeds

1 teaspoon cumin seeds

2 tablespoons olive oil

1 onion, finely chopped

2 garlic cloves, crushed

1 teaspoon ground cinnamon

¼–½ teaspoon cayenne pepper

10 oz. ground lamb

a pinch of salt

2 tablespoons chopped cilantro

4 pita breads

a few salad greens

plain yogurt

1 tablespoon sesame seeds, toasted in a dry skillet

lamb in pita bread

Say goodbye to greasy late-night takeout horrors and hello to this fresh, fast, and fantastic alternative. You'll never look back.

Put the coriander and cumin seeds into a small skillet without oil and fry until they start to brown and release their aroma. Let cool slightly, then grind to powder with a mortar and pestle.

Heat the oil in a skillet, add the onion, garlic, and ground spices, and fry gently for 5 minutes until softened but not golden. Increase the heat, add the lamb and the pinch of salt, and stir-fry for 5–8 minutes until well browned. Stir in the cilantro.

Meanwhile, lightly toast the pita bread and cut a long slit in the side of each one. Carefully fill with a few salad greens, add the ground lamb mixture, a spoonful of yogurt, and sprinkle with sesame seeds. Serve hot.

8 oz. sausages

1 onion, finely chopped

2 garlic cloves, crushed

2 ripe tomatoes, seeded and finely chopped

⅓ cup olive oil

1 cup frozen peas, defrosted

4 small flour tortillas

3 tablespoons mascarpone

1 small egg, beaten

salt and black pepper

a pastry brush

pea, sausage, and *onion* calzone

In fact, this is a cheat's calzone—made with tortillas, filled and folded over to look like calzone. Lighter and quicker to make.

Cut away the skins of the sausages and pull the sausage meat into chunks. Heat 3 tablespoons of the olive oil in a saucepan and fry the onion and garlic over gentle heat for 3–4 minutes, until the onion is starting to soften. Add the sausage meat, season with salt and pepper, and cook for 1–2 minutes, until golden. Add the tomatoes and peas and cook for 15 minutes or so, until the liquid has disappeared and the meat is cooked.

Spoon a quarter of the mixture onto one side of each tortilla, leaving a 1-inch border around the edges. Dot little bits of mascarpone over the sausage-meat mixture. Brush some beaten egg around the edge of the tortillas with a pastry brush. Fold over each tortilla to make a semi-circle. Press the edges down to seal them. Heat the remaining oil in a large skillet over medium heat and fry the tortillas for 3–4 minutes on each side, until golden. Drain on paper towels and serve.

lamb in pita bread

english breakfast pizza

Breakfast on a pizza! The portions are hearty, so make sure you have worked up a really good appetite before you start.

serves
2

M

Put the baking sheets in the oven and preheat the oven to 400°F.

Spread the mustard and ketchup over each pizza base. Arrange the tomatoes, sausages, bacon, and mushrooms on each pizza, leaving a space in the middle for the egg.

Drizzle with a little oil and carefully transfer to the hot baking sheets. Bake in the preheated oven for 15 minutes, then remove from the oven and increase the temperature to 425°F.

Crack an egg into the middle of each pizza and sprinkle with salt and pepper. Return the pizzas to the oven and cook for a further 5–10 minutes, until the egg is just set and the base is crisp and golden. Serve at once.

2 teaspoons whole-grain mustard

2 teaspoons tomato ketchup

2 x 8-inch ready-made deep pan pizza bases

5 small tomatoes, halved crosswise

6 pork chipolata sausages

6 slices of smoked bacon

5 mushrooms, halved

2 eggs

1 tablespoon olive oil

salt and black pepper

2 baking sheets

quattro stagioni pizza

The pizza for those who just can't make up their minds which one they want. You get all the best bits at once with this one.

serves
2–4

M

Put the baking sheet in the oven and preheat the oven to 400°F.

Heat 2 tablespoons of the oil in a skillet and cook the shallot for 2 minutes. Add the mushrooms and cook for a further 2–3 minutes, until softened and golden. Add salt and pepper to taste.

Brush the pizza base with a little oil. Spoon over the tomato sauce.

Pile the mushrooms over one quarter of the pizza. Arrange the ham and olives on another quarter and the artichoke hearts on the third section of pizza. Lay the mozzarella on the remaining section and put the anchovies on top.

Drizzle a little more oil over the whole pizza and sprinkle with salt and plenty of pepper. Carefully transfer to the hot baking sheet and bake in the preheated oven for 20–25 minutes, until crisp and golden. Serve at once.

¼ cup olive oil

1 shallot, thinly sliced

½ cup sliced mushrooms

12-inch ready-made deep pan pizza base

Roasted Tomato Sauce (page 125) or storebought tomato sauce

2 oz. prosciutto, shredded

6 pitted black olives

4 artichoke hearts in brine or oil, drained and quartered

3 oz. mozzarella, sliced

4 anchovy fillets in oil, drained

salt and black pepper

a baking sheet

2 x 12-inch ready-made
pizza bases (not deep pan)

2 large, ripe tomatoes,
chopped

2 tablespoons capers,
rinsed and drained

12 anchovy fillets in oil,
drained and chopped

8 oz. mozzarella, chopped

a few fresh basil leaves

salt and black pepper

2 baking sheets

tomato, caper, and anchovy pizza

Sometimes less is more, as with this pizza topping. If you have the option, use the regular rather than convection setting on your oven to make sure you get a good, crisp base on the pizza.

Put the baking sheets in the oven and preheat the oven to 400°F.

Divide the tomatoes, capers, anchovies, mozzarella, and basil leaves between the two pizza bases. Season with salt and pepper. Carefully transfer the pizzas to the hot baking sheets and bake in the preheated oven for 10–12 minutes until bubbling and golden. Serve at once.

12-inch ready-made
deep pan pizza base

2 tablespoons olive oil

Roasted Tomato Sauce
(page 125) or storebought
tomato sauce

1 large tomato, sliced

1 small red onion, sliced
and separated into rings

6 oz. mozzarella, drained
and sliced

4 oz. sliced pepperoni

salt and black pepper

a baking sheet

pepperoni pizza

Red onion, pepperoni, and melted cheese on a deep pan base—perfect Friday night comfort food.

Put the baking sheet in the oven and preheat the oven to 400°F.

Put the pizza base on the baking sheet. Brush with 1 tablespoon of the oil and spoon over the tomato sauce.

Arrange the tomato slices over the sauce. Lay the onion rings on top, splash over the remaining oil, and sprinkle with salt and plenty of pepper. Bake in the preheated oven for 20 minutes.

Remove from the oven and arrange the mozzarella and pepperoni slices over the top. Return to the oven and cook for a further 10–15 minutes, until risen and golden. Serve at once.

tomato, caper, and anchovy pizza

shrimp fried rice

shrimp fried rice

This spicy Chinese-style rice dish is packed with flavor and a great way to use up leftover basmati rice after an Indian takeout. You could also use cooked shrimp but add them after the egg.

Heat the oil in a large skillet and swirl to coat. Add the garlic, ginger, and chile and stir-fry for 30 seconds. Add the shrimp, peas, scallions, and dried shrimp and fry for 2 minutes until the fresh shrimp turn pink.

Using a spatula, push the mixture to one side, add the eggs, and scramble until set. Then add the rice and stir over high heat for 2 minutes until heated through.

Stir in the soy sauce, lemon juice, and cilantro and serve.

Note Dried shrimp are available in packages in Chinese markets. They keep very well in an airtight container.

serves 4
Q
F

2 tablespoons safflower oil

2 garlic cloves, crushed

1 inch fresh ginger, peeled and grated

1 red chile, seeded and chopped

12 oz. small uncooked shrimp, peeled, deveined, and coarsely chopped

2 cups frozen peas, defrosted

6 scallions, chopped

4 tablespoons Asian dried shrimp (see Note)

2 eggs, lightly beaten

5 cups cooked jasmine rice

3 tablespoons light soy sauce

juice of ½ lemon

2 tablespoons chopped cilantro

foil-baked *salmon* and *couscous*

Once you've put all the ingredients in the foil bag (which seals in all the flavors, making everything taste truly delicious) and popped it in the oven, there's nothing to do until 20 minutes later when it's ready to eat.

Preheat oven to 350°F.

Mix the couscous, zucchini, carrots, peas, and corn together in a bowl.

Fold a large sheet of aluminum foil or baking parchment in half and tightly fold one open side to seal. Holding the open "bag" in one hand, carefully tip in the couscous mixture. Cut the lemon in half and squeeze the juice from one half into the stock. Cut the remaining half into slices.

Lay the salmon on top of the couscous and top with the lemon slices. Tightly fold over another open side of the bag, then carefully pour in the stock. Fold the remaining open side tightly. Bake in the preheated oven for 20–25 minutes, until the fish is cooked and couscous is fluffy.

serves 2
F

1 cup couscous

2 zucchini, thinly sliced

2 carrots, finely chopped

1½ tablespoons frozen peas

1½ tablespoons corn kernels

1 unwaxed lemon

2 cups hot vegetable stock

3 salmon fillets

1 lb. dried pasta, such as tagliatelle, conchiglie, or farfalle

salt and black pepper

Tomato salad

4 firm tomatoes

3 tablespoons olive oil

1½ tablespoons chopped fresh mint or parsley

Sauce

olive oil, for cooking

2 onions, finely sliced

1 teaspoon crushed coriander seeds

12 oz. canned tuna in oil, lightly drained

1½ tablespoons capers (optional)

grated zest of 1 unwaxed lemon

½ cup milk

a handful of fresh mint sprigs, to serve

tuna, coriander, and *lemon* pasta with tomato salad

serves 4–6

F

This is a delicious lunch or dinner dish made with ingredients that, although not all strictly from the pantry, are to be found in most kitchens.

To make the tomato salad, peel the tomatoes using the instructions on page 10. Seed the tomatoes, remove the cores, and cut the flesh into small cubes. Add the oil, mint, salt, and pepper to taste and set aside to develop the flavors.

Meanwhile, cook the pasta in plenty of boiling salted water, following the manufacturer's instructions, until al dente.

To make the sauce, cover the base of a skillet with olive oil, add the onions and coriander seeds, and cook slowly over medium heat. When the onions start to soften, add 3 tablespoons water and cover with a lid. Continue cooking over low heat until soft. This will take 15 minutes—do not rush (add extra water if necessary).

When the onions are very soft, add the tuna, capers, if using, lemon zest, lots of pepper, and half the milk. Stir well, cover again, and cook for 10 minutes over low heat (add the remaining milk if necessary).

Add the sauce and the tomato salad to the freshly cooked pasta and mix well. Sprinkle with mint sprigs and serve at once.

Variation You can simply use 10 oz. cherry tomatoes, cut in half, instead of the tomato salad.

fish cakes

fish cakes

These fish cakes freeze well, so are useful if you want to get ahead with meals for the week. Any type of fish can be used.

Cook the potatoes in boiling water for 20 minutes, Drain, return to the pan, and shake over low heat to dry off. Mash the potatoes, add the butter and milk, and mix well.

Preheat the oven to 350°F.

Put the fish into the prepared dish, cover with aluminum foil, and bake for 10 minutes. Set aside to cool, then flake the fish into the potato. Beat one egg and add to the mixture, followed by the parsley, salt, and pepper. Mix well.

Put the flour, bread crumbs, and remaining eggs in 3 separate bowls. Whisk the eggs. Divide the fish mixture into 8 equal pieces and shape into patties. Dust each fish cake with flour, then use one hand to dip them into the egg; use the other hand to coat in the bread crumbs. Try to get an even coating.

Heat the oil and fry the fish cakes on each side for 5 minutes, until golden. Serve with mayonnaise.

serves **4**

F

2 lbs. potatoes, peeled

3 tablespoons butter

¼ cup milk

1 lb. salmon, cod, or halibut, skinned

3 eggs

a bunch of fresh parsley, chopped

¾ cup flour, plus extra for dusting

2 cups bread crumbs

1¼ cups olive oil

salt and black pepper

a shallow ovenproof dish, lightly greased

vegetable, seed, and nut cakes

A delicious alternative to fish cakes, especially if you have vegetarians in the house, but even non-veggies will tuck into these. It's a great way to use up leftover mashed potatoes.

Mix the mashed potatoes with the spinach in a bowl. Heat 1 tablespoon of the oil in a skillet, gently sauté the mushrooms and garlic for 5 minutes, then add to the potato mixture. Add the zucchini and season with salt and pepper, then stir well. Divide into 8 equal pieces and roll into balls.

Mix the seeds and nuts together on a large plate and roll the balls in the mixture to coat well. Gently flatten them into patties. Heat the remaining oil in a skillet and cook the patties on each side until golden, about 3–4 minutes.

serves **4**

Q

F

2½ cups mashed potatoes

1 cup cooked spinach

1¼ cups olive oil

3½ oz. mushrooms, chopped

1 garlic clove, crushed

1 zucchini, grated

¾ cup pumpkin seeds

⅛ cup sesame seeds

¾ cup peanuts, chopped

salt and black pepper

bang bang *chicken*

14 oz. ready-cooked boneless chicken, such as smoked chicken, cold roast chicken, or cold turkey

1 large carrot, peeled

salad greens such as iceberg lettuce or Chinese leaves, about 1 cup

1 cucumber, cut into matchsticks

Bang bang dressing

5 tablespoons crunchy peanut butter

1 scallion, thinly sliced

1 teaspoon sesame oil

1 teaspoon light soy sauce

1 teaspoon sugar

1 teaspoon Chinese white rice vinegar or cider vinegar

3 tablespoons hot water

serves
4

Q

M

This is a fantastic salad that's quite unusual and makes a more filling dinner than your average leafy green salad—ready-cooked smoked or "plain-roast" chicken is arranged on sticks of cucumber, then topped with a creamy peanut butter dressing.

Remove any skin from the chicken and discard. Pull or cut the chicken into shreds the size of your little finger, then put onto a plate.

Make carrot ribbons by "peeling" the carrot with a vegetable peeler to make ultra-thin long strips of carrot.

Tear any large salad greens into bite-size pieces. Arrange the greens on a serving dish. Scatter the cucumber sticks and carrot ribbons over the greens. Lastly, arrange the chicken on the top.

To make the bang bang dressing, put the peanut butter in a small bowl with the scallion. Add the sesame oil, soy sauce, sugar, vinegar, 1 teaspoon cold water, and the hot water to the bowl. Stir gently until well mixed. Taste the dressing—it should be a harmonious balance of salty, sweet, and sour flavors, so add more vinegar, sugar, or soy as you think is needed. The dressing should be just thin enough to spoon over the chicken, so if it is too thick stir in another tablespoon or so of hot water.

When the sauce seems perfect, spoon it over the chicken and serve.

new potato, crisp *salami*, and *sesame* salad

This is a world away from the kind of potato salad you buy in a plastic tub. It's really easy to prepare but packed with flavor and can be eaten on its own or, if you leave out the salami, as a side dish with Hamburgers (page 184) or Fish Cakes (page 97). It also makes a good lunchbox filler.

1 lb. 12 oz. waxy new potatoes

2 tablespoons sesame seeds

6 oz. thinly sliced salami
(a fatty, unflavored variety)

3 oz. arugula

a small bunch of fresh dill, chopped

salt and black pepper

Lemon mayonnaise

3 tablespoons mayonnaise

½ tablespoon lemon juice

To make the lemon mayonnaise, put the mayonnaise and lemon juice in a small bowl and stir well. Add a little salt and pepper.

If necessary, cut the potatoes into even-size pieces. Put in a large saucepan. Cover with cold water, add a teaspoon of salt, bring to a boil, then simmer until tender. Drain and set aside.

Heat a skillet to medium heat, add the sesame seeds and toast for about 6–8 minutes, stirring until golden. Set aside.

Reheat the skillet until hot, add the salami slices, and cook for a few minutes on each side until browned. Remove and drain on paper towels. (It will crisp up more as it cools.)

Arrange the arugula in a serving bowl. Toss the potatoes with the lemon mayonnaise and pile on top of the arugula. Scatter with half the toasted sesame seeds and dill. Crumble over the crisp salami and scatter with the remaining sesame seeds and dill to serve.

3/4 cup all-purpose flour

2 extra-large eggs

1 cup milk

a small bunch of fresh chives,
snipped into 1-inch pieces
with kitchen scissors

12 breakfast link sausages

1/4 cup vegetable oil

salt and black pepper

*a large baking sheet
or roasting pan*

2 x 6-cup muffin pans

pigs-in-a-*blanket*

serves
4–6

M

Imagine yourself back home, sitting at the dinner table with a plate of Mom's pigs-in-a-blanket in front of you. Now you can recreate this taste of home with your own super-easy pigs-in-a-blanket. They're the ideal choice for feeding famished friends.

Preheat the oven to 425°F.

Adjust the oven shelves—you will be using the middle one for the muffin pan, so make sure there is plenty of room for the batter to rise above the pan. Put a shelf under the middle one and put a large sheet or roasting pan on it to catch any drips.

To make the batter, put the flour, salt, and pepper in a large bowl. Make a hollow in the center, then break the eggs into the hollow. Pour the milk into the hollow. Using a balloon whisk, mix the eggs with the milk. Start to mix the flour into the hollow. When all the flour has been mixed in, whisk the batter well to get rid of any lumps.

Add the snipped chives and whisk them into the batter. (The batter can be made up to 3 hours before you start cooking.)

Put 1 teaspoon oil into each cup of the muffin pan, then put it into the preheated oven to heat up. Remove the pan after 5 minutes—be careful, the oil will be very, very hot—and carefully put 1 sausage in each hole, then return to the oven for 5 minutes.

Pour or ladle the batter into a large measuring cup and stir it once or twice.

Carefully remove the hot muffin pan as before, then stand back (the oil can splutter) and carefully pour the batter into each cup so each one is half full. Gently replace the pan in the oven and bake for 20 minutes until golden brown and crispy.

Remove from the oven and ease each one out of its hole with a round-bladed knife. Eat straightaway with salad or green vegetables or even baked beans.

pigs-in-a-blanket

meatloaf

meatloaf

This is very easy and tasty. It goes really well with ketchup and the Rosemary Potatoes on page 46.

Put the loaf pan on a sheet of parchment paper and draw around the base. Cut out the rectangle and lay it in the bottom of the pan to line it.

Preheat the oven to 350°F.

Put the onion, garlic, egg, ground beef, oregano, and Parmesan in a large bowl. Season well with salt and pepper.

Mix the ingredients with your fingers until everything is well combined. Spoon the mixture into the loaf pan and smooth the top with the back of a spoon. Transfer the pan to the preheated oven and cook for 45 minutes.

Remove the pan from the oven and turn the meatloaf out onto a cutting board. Cut in slices and serve with Rosemary Potatoes.

serves
4

M

1 onion, finely chopped

2 garlic cloves, crushed

1 egg, lightly beaten with a fork

2 lbs. lean ground beef

2 teaspoons dried oregano

1½ cups grated Parmesan

salt and black pepper

a 5 x 9-inch loaf pan

moussaka-filled eggplant

moussaka-filled *eggplant*

A healthy version of the Greek favorite, this looks smart but it's surprisingly fuss-free and guaranteed to please.

serves 4

M

Preheat the broiler.

Cut both eggplant in half lengthwise and scoop out the flesh with a spoon, leaving a shell approximately ¼ inch thick. Cut the eggplant flesh into small dice and set aside for the filling. Rub the oil into the eggplant shells and season the flesh lightly, then put under the broiler for 5–6 minutes until golden brown and slightly softened. Transfer to the baking sheet.

Preheat the oven to 400°F.

Put the lamb, onion, and garlic in a nonstick skillet and dry-fry over high heat for 5 minutes. Mix in the eggplant flesh, cinnamon, mint, tomato paste, and 6 tablespoons cold water, season with salt and pepper, and cook for 5 minutes. Spoon the lamb filling into the eggplant shells. Mix the yogurt with the egg yolk, nutmeg, and seasoning, then pour this over the filling. Top with the sliced tomatoes and bake in the preheated oven for 20 minutes.

2 eggplant

1 teaspoon olive oil

10 oz. lean ground lamb

1 onion, finely chopped

2 garlic cloves, crushed

1 teaspoon ground cinnamon

1 teaspoon dried mint

1 tablespoon tomato paste

Topping

⅔ cup Greek yogurt

1 egg yolk

freshly grated nutmeg

2 tomatoes, sliced

a baking sheet

pork with *sweet potato* mash

Pure comfort food! For a delicately spiced mash, stir in a teaspoon of ground cumin and half a teaspoon of hot red pepper flakes, if liked. Serve the pork with green vegetables.

serves 2

M

Mix together 1 tablespoon of the oil and the paprika and brush the mixture over the pork. Season with salt and pepper to taste.

Cook the sweet potatoes in boiling salted water until tender. Drain, then return the potatoes to the pan. Add the butter and remaining oil and mash the potatoes until smooth and creamy. Stir in the chopped cilantro and season with salt and pepper to taste.

Heat the grill pan until very hot. Grill the pork for 5–6 minutes or until cooked right through. Turn halfway and brush with more oil, if necessary.

Divide the mash between 2 plates, then top with the pork.

1½ tablespoons olive oil, plus extra if needed

½ teaspoon paprika

2 pork loin fillets, 5 oz. each

salt and black pepper

Sweet potato mash

1 lb. sweet potatoes, peeled and cut into chunks

2 teaspoons butter

4 tablespoons chopped cilantro

a ridged grill pan

vegetarian entrées

pasta and bean soup

pasta and *bean* soup

This hearty soup of pasta and beans is a classic from the region of Puglia in Italy. Beans, pasta, and potato all contribute to making it extra tasty and satisfying.

Heat the oil in a large saucepan, add the onion, garlic, and potato, and cook for 3–4 minutes until golden. Add the tomatoes and cook for 2–3 minutes until softened.

Add the stock, herbs, beans, pasta, red pepper flakes, salt, and pepper. Bring to a boil, then simmer for about 10 minutes, until the pasta and potatoes are cooked.

Ladle into bowls and serve sprinkled with a little Parmesan.

2 tablespoons olive oil

1 small onion, finely chopped

2 garlic cloves, crushed

1 potato, diced

2 ripe tomatoes, chopped

5 cups hot vegetable stock

a sprig of fresh thyme

2 x 14-oz. cans cannellini beans, drained

6 oz. dried pasta, such as orecchiette

a pinch of hot red pepper flakes

salt and black pepper

grated Parmesan, to serve

summer *minestrone*

A very light, fragrant version of a soup that can sometimes be rather heavy. It has added taste thanks to the last-minute addition of pesto.

Bring a large saucepan of water to a boil. Add a good pinch of salt, then the pasta, and cook until al dente, or according to the manufacturer's instructions. Drain well.

Meanwhile, heat the oil in another large saucepan, add the onion and garlic, and cook gently for 3 minutes. Add the celery and carrots and cook for a further 2 minutes. Add the tomatoes and cook for 2 minutes.

Add the stock and beans, bring to a boil, then simmer for 5–10 minutes, until the vegetables are cooked and tender.

Add the drained pasta, stir in the pesto, and add salt and pepper to taste. Ladle into bowls, sprinkle with Parmesan, and serve.

½ cup small dried pasta shapes, such as stellete

1 tablespoon olive oil

1 red onion, chopped

1 garlic clove, crushed

2 celery stalks, thinly sliced

5 oz. carrots, thinly sliced

2 tomatoes, chopped

5 cups hot vegetable stock

5 oz. runner or green beans, thinly sliced

2 tablespoons pesto

salt and black pepper

1 tablespoon grated Parmesan, to serve

3 tablespoons butter

2 carrots, finely chopped

2 leeks, white part only, thinly sliced

1 large onion, finely chopped

3 garlic cloves, sliced

½ teaspoon hot red pepper flakes

2 teaspoons dried oregano

14-oz. can chopped tomatoes

1 cup Puy lentils

4 cups hot vegetable stock

salt and black pepper

grated pecorino or Parmesan, to serve

crusty bread, toasted and buttered, to serve

puy lentil and *vegetable* soup

Puy lentils, which are grown in France, are very fashionable but they are also great at thickening soups without turning sludgy. They are a useful ingredient to have in your kitchen and a particularly popular, filling side dish for vegetarians.

Melt the butter in a large casserole dish or heavy-based saucepan. Add the carrots, leeks, onion, and garlic and a large pinch of salt. Stir until everything is coated in butter and cook over medium heat, with the lid on, for 15 minutes, stirring occasionally.

Once the vegetables have softened, add the red pepper flakes, oregano, tomatoes, lentils, and stock. Cover again and let simmer for 30 minutes, or until the lentils are cooked. Season with salt and pepper to taste.

Transfer to bowls and serve with buttered toast and grated pecorino or Parmesan on the side.

2 tablespoons olive oil

1 unwaxed lemon

1 onion, chopped

3 tablespoons chopped fresh flatleaf parsley

1 lb. zucchini, sliced

10 oz. frozen fava beans

3 cups hot vegetable stock

salt and black pepper

zucchini, fava bean, and *lemon* broth

To make this broth more substantial, you can add a scoop of risotto rice at the same time as the fava beans and a little more stock to compensate. Frozen fava beans are a godsend and can be added to soups, risottos, pasta, and lots more besides.

Heat the olive oil in a large saucepan. Peel the zest from the lemon in one large piece so it's easy to find later and add that to the pan. Add the onion, parsley, and zucchini, cover, and cook over low heat, stirring occasionally, for 8 minutes or until softening.

Remove the lemon zest. Add the fava beans and stock, season well with salt and pepper, and return to the heat for a further 20 minutes.

Transfer a quarter of the soup to a blender, if you have one, and liquidize until smooth, then stir back into the soup. Skip this step if you don't have a blender. Check the seasoning and add lemon juice to taste.

Ladle the soup into bowls and serve with a fresh grinding of pepper.

*puy lentil and
vegetable soup*

kitchen garden
soup

kitchen garden soup

An old-fashioned nourishing soup, full of healthy green things. If you can't find sorrel in your supermarket, leave it out.

serves 4–6

V

Put the bay leaf in a large saucepan of water and bring to a boil. Add the cabbage quarters and blanch for 3 minutes. Drain the cabbage, pat dry, and slice it thinly.

Heat the butter in a large saucepan. Add the cabbage, leeks, onion, and 2 teaspoons salt and cook until softened, 5–10 minutes. Add the potatoes, parsley, and 2 quarts water. Add salt and pepper to taste and simmer gently for 40 minutes.

Stir in the peas, lettuce, and sorrel and cook for 10 minutes more. Taste for seasoning. Ladle into bowls, add 1 tablespoon of butter to each, and serve.

1 dried bay leaf

1 small cabbage, quartered

4 tablespoons butter, plus extra to serve

2 leeks, halved and sliced

1 onion, chopped

8 oz. new potatoes, chopped

a handful of fresh flatleaf parsley, chopped

2 cups frozen peas

1 romaine lettuce heart, quartered and sliced thinly

a bunch of fresh sorrel, sliced

salt and black pepper

creamy *tomato* and *bread* soup

This is one of the most comforting soups on earth and has its origins in Italian peasant thrift. Leftover bread is never thrown away in Tuscany—here, it thickens a rich tomato soup, which is in turn enriched with Parmesan.

serves 6

V

Heat the stock slowly in a large saucepan. Meanwhile, heat the oil in a second large saucepan, add the onion and tomatoes, and fry over gentle heat for about 10 minutes until soft. Push the mixture through a strainer and stir into the hot broth. Add the bread and garlic.

Cover and simmer gently for about 45 minutes until thick and creamy, whisking from time to time to break up the bread. Take care, because this soup can stick to the bottom of the pan.

To finish, stir the Parmesan into the soup, then add salt and pepper to taste. Ladle into bowls and trickle 2 tablespoons olive oil over each serving. Serve hot, warm, or cold (but never chilled), with more Parmesan separately.

6 cups hot vegetable stock

¼ cup olive oil, plus extra to drizzle

1 onion, chopped

2½ lbs. very ripe, soft tomatoes, roughly chopped

10 oz. stale white bread, thinly sliced, crusts removed (or bread crumbs)

3 garlic cloves, crushed

1¼ cups grated Parmesan, plus extra to serve

salt and black pepper

minestrone

8 oz. smoked bacon, cut into strips (optional)

2 garlic cloves, crushed

2 large stalks of fresh parsley, lightly crushed

1 tablespoon olive oil

1 large onion, chopped

2 large potatoes, cubed and rinsed

3 carrots, cubed

2 celery stalks, sliced

3 tomatoes, halved, seeded, and chopped

1 cup risotto rice

1 small round cabbage, quartered, cored, and sliced

14-oz. can cannellini beans, drained and rinsed

2 cups frozen peas

3 small zucchini, halved lengthwise, halved again into quarters, then thickly sliced

salt and black pepper

a handful of fresh basil, torn, to serve

crusty bread, to serve

grated Parmesan, to serve

serves
6–8

V

There are as many versions of minestrone (big soup) as there are regions of Italy—and Italian grandmothers. Tomatoes, garlic, oil, and pasta are used in southern recipes, beans in soups from central Italy, and rice in the north. In Genoa they add a spoonful of pesto, in Tuscany the soup is poured over their chunky unsalted bread, and in other areas, pork in various forms is added. Leave out the bacon for a veggie soup.

Put the bacon, if using, garlic, and parsley in a large saucepan, heat gently, and fry for 5–7 minutes. Add the olive oil, heat briefly, then add the onion and cook gently until softened but not browned.

Add the potatoes, carrots, celery, tomatoes, salt, and pepper. Add 3 quarts water and heat until simmering. Cook over low heat for about 20 minutes.

Add the rice and simmer for 10 minutes. Add the cabbage, bring to a boil, and cook for 5 minutes, then add the cannellini beans, peas, and zucchini. Cook for another 2–3 minutes until all the vegetables are tender.

Remove and discard the parsley stalks, add salt and pepper to taste, then serve sprinkled with torn basil. Crusty bread and grated Parmesan are the perfect accompaniments.

Note Remember that canned beans often have sugar and salt added, so keep that in mind when you season the finished soup.

minty *pea risotto* soup

This is a cross between a soup and a risotto and should be soupy in consistency. It's a good option when your kitchen is a bit of a barren wasteland—you're bound to have a bag of peas in the freezer and the other ingredients are easy to buy. There is, in fact, pancetta in here, but do just leave it out if you're vegetarian. It will taste just as fabulous.

serves
4–6

V

2 tablespoons butter

1 onion, finely chopped

5 oz. pancetta, cubed (optional)

1¾ cups frozen peas, defrosted

2 tablespoons olive oil, plus extra for drizzling

¾ cup risotto rice

6 cups hot vegetable stock, plus extra if necessary

2 tablespoons fresh mint, shredded

salt and black pepper

grated Parmesan, to serve

Melt the butter in a medium saucepan, then add the onion and pancetta, if using. Cook over low/medium heat, with the lid on, for 8 minutes, or until the onion is softened and translucent. Stir occasionally.

Meanwhile, put half the peas in a food processor with the olive oil and blend until puréed. If you don't have a food processor, roughly mash the peas with the oil in a bowl using a fork.

Add the rice to the softening onion and stir until well coated in butter. Pour in the stock and add the puréed peas. Simmer, uncovered, for 15 minutes.

Add the remaining peas, season with salt and pepper, and cook for a further 8–10 minutes, or until the rice is tender. Stir in the mint and add a little more stock if you think it needs to be soupier.

Transfer to bowls, drizzle with olive oil, and grind over some pepper. Serve with grated Parmesan.

1 tablespoon vegetable oil

2 teaspoons sesame oil

2 garlic cloves, crushed

4 scallions, finely chopped

2 teaspoons finely grated
fresh ginger

1 small red chile, seeded
and thinly sliced

½ cup long grain white rice

6 cups hot vegetable stock

1 tablespoon soy sauce

a bunch of collard greens,
roughly shredded

a small bunch of cilantro,
chopped

white pepper

garlic and *chile* rice soup

serves
2

V

This is a substantial soup—really more of a light stew. Boiled rice soups are popular in many Asian countries, especially China where they are called congees. The greens work very nicely with the simple Asian flavors here.

Put the oils in a saucepan and set over high heat. Add the garlic and scallions and cook until the garlic is turning golden and just starting to burn. This will give the soup a lovely, nutty garlic flavor. Add the ginger, chile, and rice to the pan and stir-fry in the garlic-infused oil for 1 minute. Add the stock and soy sauce and bring to a boil.

Cover with a lid and cook over low heat for 30 minutes, until the rice is soft and the soup has thickened. Add the collard greens and cook for 5 minutes, until they turn emerald green and are tender. Ladle the soup into bowls, sprinkle the cilantro over the top, and season to taste with white pepper.

3 tablespoons red miso paste

1 tablespoon soy sauce

½ teaspoon sugar

5 cups hot vegetable stock

200 g ramen or thin egg noodles

1 tablespoon olive oil

2 teaspoons sesame oil

2 teaspoons finely sliced
fresh ginger

2 shallots, thinly sliced

2 leeks, very finely chopped

7 oz. Savoy cabbage leaves,
finely shredded

7 oz. red cabbage, finely
shredded

miso soup with *ramen noodles* and stir-fried *vegetables*

serves
4

Q

V

Japanese broths are generally made with a base of stock and soy sauce or miso. Miso (soybean paste) is probably the most essential Japanese food and easily found in the Asian foods aisle at your supermarket. It will keep for ages in the fridge.

Combine the miso, soy sauce, sugar, and stock in a large saucepan set over medium heat and warm until the miso has completely dissolved. Keep warm over low heat. Cook the noodles according to the manufacturer's instructions. Drain well and divide between 4 bowls.

Put the oils in a large skillet over high heat. Add the ginger and shallots and cook for just a few seconds to flavor the oil. Add the leeks and cabbage and stir-fry for 2 minutes, until crisp and glistening with oil.

Ladle the warm miso mixture over the noodles and top with the stir-fried vegetables. Serve immediately.

miso soup with ramen noodles
and stir-fried vegetables

spaghetti with *garlic, olive oil,* and *chile* sauce

12 oz. dried pasta, such spaghetti or linguine

grated Parmesan (optional), to serve

Garlic, olive oil, and chile sauce

⅔ cup olive oil

4 garlic cloves, peeled but whole

1 teaspoon hot red pepper flakes

2 handfuls of fresh parsley, finely chopped

serves
4–6

Q

V

If you like spicy and ridiculously simple food, this is for you. Make this dressing swiftly, cook the pasta al dente, use the best-quality ingredients, and serve straightaway. Apart from the fresh parsley, you only need things you are likely to have lurking in your kitchen cupboards already. If not, buy them and know that you will always have the means to make this fantastic pasta dish, no matter how empty your fridge is.

Bring a large saucepan of water to a boil. Add a good pinch of salt, then the pasta, and cook until al dente, or according to the manufacturer's instructions.

While the pasta is boiling, slowly heat the olive oil in a skillet with the garlic and red pepper flakes. When the garlic turns golden, discard it. Drain the pasta, then return it to the saucepan. Add the hot flavored oil and chopped parsley and stir well. Serve at once, with Parmesan, if using.

Variation For spice lovers, arrabbiata is a tomato-based version of the recipe above. The word arrabbiata means "rabid" and is used in Italian to mean "angry." It is a popular dish in Rome and generally made on demand in simple eateries. To make a simplified arrabbiata, use the Roasted Tomato Sauce recipe on page 125, but double the amount of garlic and hot red pepper flakes and replace the basil with parsley.

spaghetti with garlic, olive oil, and chile sauce

penne with broccoli and pine nut pesto

penne with *broccoli* and *pine nut* pesto

This can be rustled up in a matter of minutes. All you need is fresh broccoli and a few basic ingredients and you have the makings of a fine TV dinner.

Bring a large saucepan of water to a boil. Add a good pinch of salt, then the pasta, and cook until al dente, or according to the manufacturer's instructions. Cook the broccoli in a separate saucepan of boiling, salted water for 10–12 minutes until very soft.

Meanwhile, heat a dry skillet until hot, add the pine nuts, and cook, turning them frequently, until golden and toasted. Set aside.

Heat the olive oil in a small saucepan and add the garlic and chile. Gently cook for 2–3 minutes until softened. Remove from the heat and set aside.

Drain the broccoli, return it to the pan, and mash coarsely with a fork.

Drain the pasta and return it to the warm pan. Add the mashed broccoli, garlic, and chile oil, and toasted pine nuts. Mix well, squeeze in a little lemon juice, and add salt and pepper to taste. Top with Parmesan shavings.

serves
2

6 oz. dried pasta, such as penne or fusilli

6 oz. broccoli, cut into florets

2 tablespoons pine nuts

3 tablespoons olive oil

3 garlic cloves, crushed

1 red chile, seeded and finely chopped

½ a lemon

Parmesan shavings, to serve

salt and black pepper

pasta with roasted
eggplant and tomato

pasta with *roasted* *eggplant* and *tomato*

A vegetarian pasta with the beefy substance of eggplant. It needs time in the oven, so you can get on with something else.

serves 4

V

2 eggplant, cut into 1-inch cubes

1¼ lbs. ripe tomatoes, quartered

2 garlic cloves, halved

¼ cup olive oil

10 oz. dried pasta, such as fusilli or penne

1 shallot, finely chopped

2 tablespoons chopped fresh mint

2 tablespoons chopped cilantro

juice of 1 lime

salt and black pepper

Preheat the oven to 400°F.

Put the eggplant, tomatoes, and garlic into a large roasting pan. Add 2 tablespoons of the oil and mix. Sprinkle with salt and pepper and cook in the preheated oven for 30–40 minutes, turning the vegetables from time to time, until the eggplant is tender and golden.

Meanwhile, bring a large saucepan of water to a boil. Add a good pinch of salt, then the pasta, and cook until al dente, or according to the manufacturer's instructions.

Drain the pasta well and return it to the warm pan. Add the roasted eggplant and tomatoes, then the shallot, mint, cilantro, and lime juice. Add the remaining oil and toss well to mix.

three-cheese baked penne

A simplified version of that old-time favorite, macaroni and cheese, but with no flour and no risk of lumps.

serves 4

V

12 oz. dried pasta, such as penne or macaroni

2 cups mascarpone

2 tablespoons whole-grain mustard

10 oz. Fontina cheese, grated

4 tablespoons grated Parmesan

salt and black pepper

an ovenproof dish

Bring a large saucepan of water to a boil. Add a good pinch of salt, then the pasta, and cook until al dente, or according to the manufacturer's instructions. Meanwhile, preheat the oven to 400°F.

Drain the pasta well and return it to the warm pan. Add the mascarpone and stir to mix. Add the mustard, Fontina, and Parmesan, with salt and pepper to taste. Stir to mix.

Transfer to the ovenproof dish and cook in the preheated oven for 25–30 minutes until golden and bubbling.

pasta with *ricotta, cherry tomatoes,* and *basil*

3 tablespoons salt

1 lb. dried pasta, such as farfalle, fusilli, or penne

1 pint ripe cherry tomatoes

about 1 cup ricotta, drained

⅓ cup olive oil

a large handful of fresh basil leaves, sliced

grated Parmesan, to serve

salt and black pepper

serves 4–6
Q
V

You could almost call this a salad, but it's not; it's pasta with an uncooked sauce. It is just the thing when temperatures soar, because it is light but still substantial.

Bring a large saucepan of water to a boil. Add a good pinch of salt, then the pasta, and cook until al dente, or according to the manufacturer's instructions.

Meanwhile, halve or quarter the tomatoes, depending on their size. Put in a large, shallow bowl and crumble in the ricotta. Add the oil, basil, and about ½ teaspoon salt. Mix well and set aside.

When the pasta is cooked, drain well, then add to the bowl with the tomatoes, 2–3 tablespoons grated Parmesan, and some pepper. Toss well. Add more salt and/or Parmesan to taste. Serve warm or at room temperature, with extra Parmesan and pepper.

noodle mountain

12 oz. dried egg noodles

⅓ cup canola oil

4 garlic cloves, crushed

5 inches fresh ginger, peeled and finely chopped

4 onions, finely sliced

4 chiles, finely chopped

1 Chinese cabbage, finely shredded

8 oz. bean sprouts

¾ cup soy sauce

juice of 4 limes

2 bunches of scallions, chopped

14 oz. cashew nuts, chopped

serves 10
Q
V

Throwing a party? Need something quick, stress-free, and vegetarian-friendly? Here's your answer—a noodle mountain to feed at least 10 people. Other vegetables can always be added, such as asparagus, baby corn, thin green beans, carrots, mushrooms, or water chestnuts.

Cook the noodles according to the manufacturer's instructions, drain, and transfer to a bowl of cold water until needed.

Heat the oil in a large skillet and add the garlic, ginger, onions, and chiles. Cook over medium heat for 5 minutes until softened. Add the cabbage and bean sprouts and stir briefly. Drain the noodles well and add to the skillet. Toss with 2 large spoons, then add the soy sauce, lime juice, scallions, and cashew nuts. Mix well and serve.

*pasta with ricotta,
cherry tomatoes, and basil*

roasted tomato sauce

roasted tomato sauce

This is the ultimate tomato sauce—the tomatoes are roasted first to give them a really sweet flavor. Master this and you'll be serving it with spaghetti, as part of vegetable lasagne, or as a pizza topping, as well as having a base for soups or stews.

Preheat the oven to 450°F.

Put the tomatoes, olive oil, garlic, lemon zest, red pepper flakes, and seasoning in a roasting pan in a single layer. Toss well. Roast in the preheated oven for 45 minutes, or until the tomatoes are browned and the juices reduced to a glaze.

Transfer the tomatoes and all the pan juices to a deep bowl, add the basil and, using a stick blender, purée until smooth. Season to taste. Serve hot with some freshly cooked pasta or let cool in a plastic container.

serves
4

V

2¼ lbs. vine-ripened tomatoes, roughly chopped

2 tablespoons olive oil

2 garlic cloves, crushed

grated zest of
1 unwaxed lemon

a pinch of hot red pepper flakes

2 tablespoons chopped fresh basil

salt and black pepper

a roasting pan

¼ cup safflower oil

1 garlic clove, crushed

2 inches fresh ginger, peeled and finely chopped

1 onion, thinly sliced

1 chile, finely chopped

4 oz. egg noodles

2 bok choy, roughly chopped

1 leek, cut into strips

1½ cups bean sprouts, trimmed

1½ cups sliced mushrooms

3 tablespoons soy sauce

juice of 1 lime

a bunch of cilantro, chopped

vegetable noodle stir-fry

serves **4**

Q

V

When making this dish, prepare the ingredients in advance, so the stir-fry can be quickly put together. You can vary the vegetables but always use the onion, garlic, ginger, and chile.

Heat the oil in a large skillet. Add the garlic, ginger, onion, and chile and cook over medium heat, stirring constantly.

Bring a large saucepan of water to a boil. Add the noodles and cook according to the manufacturer's instructions. Drain thoroughly.

Add the bok choy, leek, bean sprouts, and mushrooms to the skillet and stir-fry for 2–3 minutes.

Add the soy sauce, lime juice, and noodles and use 2 spoons to mix the vegetables and noodles together. Top with the chopped cilantro and serve immediately.

bell peppers stuffed with pasta

4 yellow or red bell peppers

2 oz. very fine spaghetti, broken into pieces

½ cup olive oil

12 ripe cherry tomatoes, quartered

2 garlic cloves, crushed

3 tablespoons chopped fresh basil

½ cup pine nuts, chopped

½ teaspoon hot red pepper flakes (optional)

1 cup grated pecorino or Parmesan

salt and black pepper

a baking dish, lightly greased

serves **4**

V

These bell peppers are a vegetable and pasta course in one. They should be soft, with a wrinkled, browned exterior. The garlicky cherry tomatoes help to keep the pasta moist.

Slice the tops off the bell peppers and reserve. Scrape out and discard all the seeds and white pith. Set the peppers upright in the baking dish small enough to fit them snugly. If they don't stand upright, shave a little piece off the base, but not right through.

Bring a saucepan of water to a boil. Add a good pinch of salt, then the pasta, and cook until al dente, or according to the manufacturer's instructions. Drain well and toss with 2 tablespoons of the olive oil. Meanwhile, preheat the oven to 425°F.

Put the tomatoes in a bowl with another 2 tablespoons of oil, the garlic, basil, pine nuts, red pepper flakes, and pecorino and mix well. Add the pasta to the peppers, filling them by two-thirds, then spoon in the tomato mixture. Put the lids on top and brush all over with the remaining olive oil. Bake in the preheated oven for 25–30 minutes or until the peppers start to wrinkle.

bell peppers
stuffed with pasta

pea and *parmesan* risotto

Making a risotto is simple, but it takes time and risotto rice needs constant stirring as it cooks. Look for risotto rice called arborio, carnaroli, and vialone nano in the supermarket.

Heat the olive oil in a medium, heavy-based pan over very low heat and stir in the onion and garlic. Cook gently for about 10 minutes until the onion is translucent but not yet brown. Stir in the rice and make sure it is well coated in oil, then stir in the peas.

Turn up the heat to medium and add a ladle of the hot vegetable stock. Stir gently and as soon as the liquid is absorbed by the rice, add another ladle of stock.

Keep on stirring the rice gently and continuously so it doesn't stick to the the pan, and keep on adding the hot stock. It will take about 20 minutes of stirring before the rice is tender. Taste a few grains with a teaspoon. The mixture should be creamy and moist, but not dry or very wet and soupy— the exact amount of stock you will need depends on the brand of rice you use and how fast the rice is cooking.

As soon as the rice is tender, turn off the heat. Add the butter, salt, and pepper to taste, plus half the Parmesan. Stir gently into the rice, then cover the pan and leave for 4–5 minutes.

Sprinkle the parsley on top, then serve with the remaining Parmesan.

2 tablespoons olive oil

1 onion, finely chopped

2 garlic cloves, crushed

1⅛ cups risotto rice

1¼ cups frozen peas

about 3 cups hot vegetable stock

1 tablespoon butter

1 cup grated Parmesan

salt and black pepper

chopped fresh flatleaf parsley, to serve

butternut squash, sage, and *chile* risotto

about 6 cups hot
vegetable stock

1 stick butter

1 large onion, finely chopped

1–2 fresh or dried red chiles,
seeded and finely chopped

1¼ lbs. butternut squash
or pumpkin (or swede),
peeled and finely diced

2 cups risotto rice

3 tablespoons chopped
fresh sage

¾ cup grated Parmesan

salt and black pepper

serves
6

V

This tastes wonderful on its own—it's filling and delicious as a vegetarian entrée—but you could also serve it in smaller portions for meat-eaters as a side with broiled lamb chops. Buying fresh sage just for this dish may seem like an extravagance but in fact sage leaves freeze very well: wash and pat them dry, then pop them loose in a freezer bag and freeze for up to 1 year. Note that the flavor becomes even more intense when the leaves are frozen so use them in moderation.

Pour the stock into a saucepan and keep at a gentle simmer. Melt half the butter in a large, heavy saucepan and add the onion. Cook gently for 10 minutes until soft, golden, and translucent but not browned. Stir in the chopped chiles and cook for 1 minute. Add the butternut squash, and cook, stirring constantly over the heat for 5 minutes, until it begins to soften slightly. Stir in the rice to coat with the butter and vegetables. Cook for a few minutes to toast the grains.

Begin adding the stock, a large ladle at a time, stirring gently until each ladle has almost been absorbed by the rice. The risotto should be kept at a bare simmer throughout cooking, so don't let the rice dry out—add more stock as necessary. Continue until the rice is tender and creamy, but the grains still firm and the squash beginning to disintegrate. (This should take 15–20 minutes depending on the type of rice used—check the manufacturer's instructions.)

Taste and season well with salt and pepper, then stir in the sage, remaining butter, and all the Parmesan. Cover and let rest for a couple of minutes, then serve.

parmesan and
butter risotto

parmesan and *butter* risotto

Even if you have desperately bare kitchen cupboards and fridge, you're likely to have what's needed for this comforting risotto.

serves
4–6

V

Put the stock in a saucepan and keep at a gentle simmer. Melt half the butter in a large, heavy saucepan and add the onion. Cook gently for 10 minutes until soft, golden, and translucent but not browned. Add the rice and stir until well coated with the butter and heated through. Pour in the wine and boil hard until it has reduced and almost disappeared. This will remove any raw alcohol taste.

Begin adding the stock, a large ladle at a time, stirring gently until each ladle has almost been absorbed by the rice. Don't let the rice dry out—add more stock as necessary. Continue until the rice is tender and creamy, but the grains still firm. (This should take 15–20 minutes depending on the type of rice used—check the manufacturer's instructions.) Taste and season well with salt and pepper, then stir in the remaining butter and all the Parmesan. Cover and let rest until the cheese has melted, then serve.

about 6 cups hot vegetable stock

1 stick plus 2 tablespoons butter

1 onion, finely chopped

2 cups risotto rice

⅔ cup dry white wine

1 cup grated Parmesan

salt and black pepper

risotto primavera

This is a chance to use up fresh spring vegetables. The choice is yours but make sure they're are at their freshest and greenest.

serves
4

V

Heat the butter and olive oil in a large saucepan. Add the onion and garlic and cook over low heat for 5 minutes until softened and translucent. Add the rice, stirring with a wooden spoon to coat the grains thoroughly with butter and oil. Add a ladle of stock to the rice, mix well, and let simmer. When the liquid has almost evaporated, add another ladle of stock and stir thoroughly until it bubbles away. Continue stirring the risotto as often as possible and adding more stock as needed.

After the risotto has been cooking for 12 minutes, add all the vegetables and mix well. Add the remaining stock, white wine, salt, and pepper. Cook, stirring, for a further 4–5 minutes, then mix in the chopped parsley and grated Parmesan.

7 tablespoons butter

3 tablespoons olive oil

1 onion, diced

1 garlic clove, crushed

1¼ cups risotto rice

about 4 cups hot vegetable stock

1¼ lbs. mixed green vegetables, such as green beans, runner beans, fava beans, green cabbage, peas, or spinach, all chopped into evenly-sized pieces

⅓ cup white wine

a bunch of fresh flatleaf parsley, chopped

1¼ cups grated Parmesan

salt and black pepper

2 tablespoons olive oil

1 onion, chopped

1 garlic clove, crushed

1½ cups risotto rice

2 tablespoons fresh
rosemary needles

2 zucchini, roughly chopped

2 tomatoes, chopped

3 cups hot vegetable stock

3 tablespoons butter

½ cup grated Parmesan

*a flameproof, lidded
casserole dish*

zucchini and tomato risotto

serves
4

V

This risotto is baked in the oven, which means you are not going to get the creamy texture of one cooked conventionally. However, the good thing is that it doesn't need constant stirring.

Preheat the oven to 400°F.

Put the oil in the casserole dish and set over low heat. Add the onion and garlic and fry gently for 2–3 minutes until the onion has softened. Add the rice and rosemary and cook for 1 minute before adding the zucchini. Stir for 1 minute, or until the rice becomes opaque, then add the tomatoes. Pour the hot stock into the casserole and stir well to combine all the ingredients. As soon as the liquid starts to simmer, cover with the lid and cook in the preheated oven for 30 minutes. Stir through the butter and half of the Parmesan, then sprinkle the remaining Parmesan on top to serve.

couscous with feta, dill, and spring beans

1¾ cups couscous

1¾ cups hot water

½ cup olive oil

1 garlic clove, crushed

3 shallots, thinly sliced

2 tablespoons chopped
fresh dill

2 tablespoons snipped
fresh chives

1 tablespoon zest and flesh of
fresh lemon, finely chopped

8 oz. feta cheese, chopped

5 oz. sugar snap peas

5 oz. frozen baby fava beans,
defrosted

5 oz. frozen peas, defrosted

black pepper

serves
4

Q

V

Marinating the feta in this fresh-tasting salad lifts it from a salty, creamy cheese to something much more complex, so it's well worth it, even if it's just for 5 minutes.

Put the couscous in a large bowl and pour over the hot water. Cover with plastic wrap or a plate and let swell for 10 minutes.

Pour the olive oil into a mixing bowl and add the garlic, shallots, dill, chives, and lemon zest and flesh and lots of black pepper—the coarser the better. Add the feta, turn in the oil, and set aside while you cook the beans.

Bring a medium saucepan of unsalted water to a boil. Add the sugar snap peas, bring back to a boil, and cook for 1 minute. Add the fava beans, bring back to a boil, and cook for 1 minute. Finally, add the peas and cook for 2 minutes. Drain.

Uncover the couscous, stir in the hot beans, transfer to bowls, and top with the feta, spooning over the flavored oil as you go. Stir well before serving.

couscous with feta, dill, and spring beans

moroccan-style
roasted vegetable couscous

Couscous is an excellent pantry staple for the busy cook as it doesn't need cooking—it is simply soaked in hot water or stock and fluffed up with a fork. It is classically served with a rich North African stew called a tagine, named after the dish with the conical lid in which it is cooked. The couscous acts like an absorbent sponge and mops up the sauce. This roasted vegetable couscous is spicy and satisfying. If time is very short, look out for pre-packed, peeled, and chopped vegetables from supermarkets but beware that they will be more expensive.

Preheat the oven to 400°F.

Remove the thin skin from the onions and slice them into thin wedges. Peel the sweet potato and cut into chunks. Core and seed the bell peppers, then chop. Trim the leeks, then split them and wash well. Dry with paper towels and cut into large chunks.

Put the prepared vegetables and garlic on the baking sheet or in the small roasting pan. Pour the olive oil over the top, add the red pepper flakes, and use your hands to toss the vegetables until they are coated with the oil mixture. Place the sheet or pan in the preheated oven and cook for about 20–25 minutes, or until golden and tender.

Meanwhile, put the couscous in a large bowl and pour over the hot stock or water. Cover with plastic wrap or a plate and let swell for 10 minutes.

Use a fork to fluff up the couscous, then add the roasted vegetables and mint sprigs. Add a little lemon juice and season with salt and pepper to taste. Serve immediately while still warm.

Variation Add 2 oz. crumbled or diced feta cheese to the couscous.

serves
2

V

2 small red onions

1 sweet potato

2 small red bell peppers

2 small leeks

2 garlic cloves, halved

2 tablespoons olive oil

½ teaspoon hot red pepper flakes

1¼ cups couscous

1¼ cups hot vegetable stock or water

a handful of fresh mint sprigs

lemon juice, to taste

salt and black pepper

a nonstick baking sheet or small roasting pan

1 onion, finely chopped

1 garlic clove, crushed

1⅔ cups hot vegetable stock

1½ cups bulgur wheat

2 teaspoons cumin seeds

1½ teaspoons ground coriander

a pinch of ground chiles

1 carrot, diced

14-oz. can chopped tomatoes

2 small zucchini, diced

6 oz. mushrooms, chopped

14-oz. can chickpeas, drained
and rinsed

6 oz. baby spinach

salt and black pepper

chickpea and *vegetable* bulgur pilau

serves
4

V

Serve this Indian-style pilau with a spoonful of plain yogurt and some chopped cilantro.

Put the onion and garlic in a large saucepan with 4 tablespoons of the stock. Cover and cook over medium heat for 5 minutes until softened.

Stir in the bulgur wheat, spices, and carrot and cook for 1–2 minutes, stirring, then add the tomatoes, zucchini, mushrooms, chickpeas, and the remaining stock. Add the salt and some pepper. Bring to a boil, then reduce the heat, cover, and simmer for 15 minutes.

Stir the pilau, pile the spinach on top, then replace the lid and cook for a further 5 minutes. Mix the cooked spinach into the pilau and serve.

broiled portobello *mushrooms*

4 large portobello or
field mushrooms

olive oil (see method)

¾ cup white wine

2 garlic cloves, crushed

juice of 1 lemon

3 tablespoons chopped
fresh parsley

salt and black pepper

serves
4

Q

V

These whole, large mushrooms are just as good served alongside a meat entrée as they are as a vegetarian appetizer. They require barely any preparation, and are broiled, on your plate, and covered in a simple sauce in a matter of minutes.

Preheat the broiler.

Pull the stalks off the mushrooms and set the caps open side up on an oiled broiler pan. Chop the stalks finely and set aside. Brush the mushrooms with olive oil, season with salt and pepper, and cook under the broiler for just 5 minutes.

Meanwhile, put 3 tablespoons olive oil in a skillet with the white wine, garlic, lemon juice, parsley, and the reserved chopped stalks. Bring to a boil, then boil hard to reduce by half. Season well and take off the heat. Transfer the mushrooms to plates and pour the sauce over the top.

*chickpea and
vegetable
bulgur pilau*

greek barley
salad

ratatouille

All the vegetables for ratatouille must be fresh and full of flavor in order to show off this famous French dish at its best.

serves
4

V

Heat the oil in a large saucepan. Add the onions and garlic and cook, stirring, for 3 minutes without browning.

Add the bell peppers, eggplant, and zucchini to the pan and cook for 5 minutes, stirring frequently. Add the canned tomatoes, oregano, and marjoram. Season generously with salt and pepper and stir thoroughly. Bring the mixture to a boil, then reduce the heat under the pan and simmer for 25 minutes, stirring occasionally.

Transfer the ratatouille to a large serving bowl. Sprinkle with the chopped parsley or basil, then drizzle with some extra olive oil and serve.

Note Try making this the day before you plan to eat it. The flavor really seems to improve overnight and benefits from being cooled and reheated.

3 tablespoons olive oil, plus extra to serve

2 onions, chopped

2 garlic cloves, crushed

2 red bell peppers, seeded and cut into chunks

2 eggplant, cut into chunks

3 zucchini, thickly sliced

2 x 14-oz. cans peeled chopped tomatoes

½ teaspoon dried oregano

½ teaspoon dried marjoram

a bunch of fresh flatleaf parsley or basil, chopped

salt and black pepper

greek *barley* salad

This hearty version of the traditional and much-loved salad incorporates satisfyingly chewy barley. If you are able to buy good-quality dried Greek oregano from specialty food stores, it will make all the difference to the flavor.

serves
4

V

Cook the barley in a saucepan of boiling salted water for 30 minutes or until tender. Drain and set aside until needed.

In a large serving bowl, whisk together the lemon juice and zest, vinegar, and oil, then stir in the warm barley and mix well. Let cool.

Soak the onion in a bowl of ice water for 10 minutes. Drain well.

Add the drained onion to the barley along with the tomatoes, cucumber, bell pepper, and olives and mix to combine. Season with salt and pepper.

Crumble the feta over the top of the salad and sprinkle with oregano.

⅔ cup pearl barley

juice and finely grated zest of 1 unwaxed lemon

2 teaspoons white or red wine vinegar

¼ cup olive oil

1 red onion, thinly sliced

4 tomatoes, chopped

1 large cucumber or 2 small (Lebanese), seeded and chopped

1 green bell pepper, seeded and chopped

20 pitted black olives

5 oz. feta cheese

1 teaspoon dried oregano

salt and black pepper

1 red onion, sliced

1 red or yellow bell pepper, seeded and sliced

1 teaspoon safflower oil

2 large mushrooms, sliced

1 garlic clove, crushed

3 teaspoons Cajun spice mix

2 tomatoes, chopped

14-oz. can pinto beans, drained and rinsed

juice of ½ an unwaxed lime

4 soft whole-wheat tortillas

4 tablespoons sour cream

1 cup shredded iceberg lettuce

salt and black pepper

bean burritos

serves 4

Q

V

This is a filling and spicy meal—good for throwing together in super-quick time. Keep plenty of serviettes handy!

Fry the onion and bell peppers in the oil for 3 minutes in a nonstick skillet. Add the mushrooms, garlic, and 2 teaspoons of the Cajun spice and stir-fry for 1 minute. Mix in the tomatoes, cover the skillet, and cook for 2 minutes.

Meanwhile, roughly mash the beans together with the remaining Cajun spice, the lime juice, and seasoning to taste.

Spread each tortilla with 1 tablespoon of the sour cream. Spoon on a quarter of the mashed beans and a quarter of the vegetable mixture. Top with shredded lettuce and roll up to serve.

1 tablespoon butter

1 tablespoon safflower oil

1 small onion, sliced

3 extra-large eggs

2 oz. firm blue cheese such as Roquefort, crumbled

salt and black pepper

a 7-inch skillet (measure the base, not the top)

onion and *blue cheese* omelet

serves 1

Q

V

A strong blue cheese, such as Roquefort, adds a powerful flavor to this omelet. However, if you prefer a more delicate flavor, use creamy dolcelatte or Gorgonzola, chopped into small pieces.

Put half the butter and oil in the skillet and heat until the butter has melted. Add the onion and fry gently for about 10 minutes, until golden and caramelized, stirring occasionally.

Meanwhile, break the eggs into a bowl and whisk briefly with a fork, just enough to mix the yolks and whites. Season with salt and pepper. Using a slotted spoon, add the onions to the eggs and mix gently.

Increase the heat to medium-high and add the remaining butter and oil. When the skillet is hot, pour in the omelet mixture. Using a spatula or the back of a fork, draw the mixture from the sides to the center as it sets. Let the liquid flow and fill the space at the sides. Sprinkle the cheese over the top, fold over a third of the omelet to the center, then fold over the remaining third. Serve immediately.

bean
burritos

*minted
zucchini
frittata*

minted *zucchini* frittata

This frittata (an Italian-style omelet) needs to be finished off under the broiler so make sure your skillet is ovenproof, and that the handle is away from the broiler's direct heat.

Cook the potatoes in a saucepan of boiling, salted water until just tender. Drain thoroughly. Meanwhile, break the eggs into a bowl and whisk briefly with a fork. Season well with salt and pepper. Mix in the chopped mint.

Meanwhile, heat the oil in the skillet, add the onion, and cook gently for about 10 minutes, until soft and pale golden. Add the zucchini and stir over low heat for 3–4 minutes until just softened. Add the potatoes and mix gently.

Preheat the broiler.

Pour the eggs over the vegetables and cook over low heat until the frittata is lightly browned underneath and has almost set on top. Slide under the broiler for 30–60 seconds, to set the top. Serve, cut into wedges.

serves 3–4

Q

V

8 oz. baby new potatoes, thickly sliced

6 extra-large eggs

2 tablespoons chopped fresh mint

2 tablespoons olive or safflower oil

1 large onion, chopped

4 zucchini, sliced

salt and black pepper

a 12-inch skillet (measure the base, not the top)

spiced *eggplant* dahl

"Dahl" literally means lentil and refers to any Indian dish of stewed, spiced lentils. This recipe uses yellow split lentils which require no soaking and cook quickly. It benefits from being made a day in advance, which gives the flavors time to mingle and mellow. Serve with steamed basmati rice or bread.

Heat the oil in a saucepan over high heat. Add the onions and stir-fry for 6–8 minutes, until they start to become golden. Reduce the heat and stir in the garlic, ginger, cumin seeds, and curry powder. Stir-fry for 1–2 minutes, then add the lentils and 2½ cups water. Bring to a boil, add the eggplant and cherry tomatoes, and reduce the heat to low. Cover and simmer gently for 25–30 minutes, stirring occasionally, until the dahl is thick and the lentils are tender.

Season well with salt and stir in the cilantro. Serve with steamed basmati rice or bread, if you like.

serves 2

V

3 tablespoons safflower oil

2 onions, finely chopped

4 garlic cloves, crushed

1 teaspoon finely grated fresh ginger

1 tablespoon cumin seeds

2 tablespoons mild curry powder

1 scant cup dried yellow split lentils

1 eggplant, cut into bite-size pieces

8 cherry tomatoes

8 tablespoons chopped cilantro

salt

12-inch ready-made
deep pan pizza base

2 tablespoons olive oil

Roasted Tomato Sauce
(page 125) or storebought
tomato sauce

7 oz. small tomatoes,
quartered or sliced

5 oz. mozzarella, sliced

salt and black pepper

a handful of fresh basil
leaves, to serve

a baking sheet

margherita pizza

serves
2–4

V

The red, white, and green on this pizza symbolize the tricolore
of the Italian flag. Since the topping is so simple, try to use
the best ingredients you can afford.

Put the baking sheet in the oven and preheat the oven to 400°F.

Brush the pizza base with half the oil. Spoon over the tomato sauce
and arrange the tomatoes and mozzarella on top.

Drizzle the pizza with the remaining oil and sprinkle with salt and
plenty of pepper. Carefully transfer to the hot baking sheet and cook
for 20–25 minutes, until crisp and golden.

Scatter the basil leaves over the hot pizza and serve.

2 red bell peppers

2 yellow bell peppers

2 garlic cloves, crushed

a small bunch of fresh flatleaf
parsley, finely chopped

3 tablespoons olive oil

Roasted Tomato Sauce
(page 125) or storebought
tomato sauce

5 oz. tomatoes, sliced
or halved

5 oz. mozzarella, sliced

salt and black pepper

a baking sheet

a small roasting pan

roasted bell pepper pizza

serves
4

V

Roasting bell peppers is a lovely way to bring out the sweetness.
Make sure they are still warm when you add the flesh to the
oil, so that they absorb the flavors of the garlic and parsley.

Put the baking sheet in the oven and preheat the oven to 425°F.

Put the bell peppers in the roasting pan and bake for 30 minutes, turning
them occasionally, until the skin blisters and blackens.

Meanwhile, put the garlic and parsley in a bowl. Add 2 tablespoons of the
olive oil and salt and pepper to taste.

Remove the peppers from the oven, cover with a clean kitchen towel, and set
aside for about 10 minutes, until cool enough to handle but still warm. Pierce
the bottom of each pepper and squeeze the juice into the oil mixture. Skin and
seed the peppers. Cut the flesh into 1-inch strips and add to the mixture.

Brush the pizza base with the remaining olive oil. Spoon over the tomato
sauce and arrange the tomatoes and mozzarella on top. Spoon the pepper
mixture over the top. Carefully transfer to the hot baking sheet and cook for
20–25 minutes, until crisp and golden.

roasted
bell pepper
pizza

food to impress

baked *pasta* with *eggplant, basil,* and *ricotta*

13 oz. dried pasta, such as rigatoni or penne

¾ cup olive oil

1 eggplant, halved and very thinly sliced

1 onion, chopped

2 garlic cloves, crushed

3 tomatoes, chopped

a small bunch of fresh basil leaves, torn

½ cup red wine

4 oz. ricotta

½ cup grated Parmesan or pecorino

salt and black pepper

an ovenproof dish

serves
4

V

This is sensible entertaining: spend a little time in the kitchen preparing the ingredients, then throw them all in an ovenproof dish and let them do their thing in the oven for 20 minutes, leaving you free to chat, open a bottle of wine, and relax. Cooking should not be stressful and this bake proves that it is possible. The sauce should be sweet and fruity so do use up any soft, overripe tomatoes. Ideally you should use a light olive oil here; extra virgin olive oil burns at a lower temperature and will make the eggplant bitter and oily.

Preheat the oven to 425°F.

Bring a large saucepan of water to a boil. Add a good pinch of salt, then the pasta, and cook until al dente, or according to the manufacturer's instructions. Drain well and return to the warm pan.

Heat the oil in a skillet and when it is hot, but not smoking, cook the eggplant slices, in batches, for 2 minutes on each side, until golden. Remove and place on paper towels. Repeat to cook all of the eggplant. Pour off all but 1 tablespoon of oil from the skillet, add the onion and garlic, and cook for 2–3 minutes, stirring often. Add the tomatoes, basil, and red wine, 1 cup water, salt, and pepper to taste and bring to a boil. Boil for 10 minutes, until you have a thickened sauce. Stir in the eggplant, then add to the pasta and stir well.

Put the mixture in the ovenproof dish. Spoon the ricotta on top, sprinkle over the Parmesan, and bake in the preheated oven for 20 minutes until golden and crispy around the edges.

pasta with *proscuitto, arugula,* and bubbling *blue cheese*

Try to find the right cheese for this pasta—it needs to be cylindrical and have a firm rind so that you can slice it in rounds. That way it will keep its shape when it is broiled.

Bring a large saucepan of water to a boil. Add a good pinch of salt, then the pasta, and cook until al dente, or according to the manufacturer's instructions.

Preheat the broiler.

Heat a little of the oil in a nonstick skillet, add the prosciutto, and cook for 1 minute on each side until crisp. Remove and drain on paper towels. Add the remaining oil to the skillet. When hot, add the cherry tomatoes and cook for 3–4 minutes until split and softened.

Meanwhile, cut each cheese in half crosswise, put cut side up under the broiler, and cook for 2–3 minutes, until golden and bubbling.

Break the prosciutto into pieces and add to the skillet. Add the Marsala, parsley, and salt and pepper to taste.

Drain the pasta well and return it to the warm pan. Add the prosciutto and tomato mixture and toss gently to mix. Divide between 4 bowls or plates and sprinkle with arugula. Using a spatula, slide a bubbling cheese half on top of each serving. Grind over some pepper and serve.

serves
4

10 oz. dried pasta, such as pappardelle or tagliatelle

2 tablespoons olive oil

8 slices of prosciutto

1 pint cherry tomatoes

2 soft blue cheeses, about 5 oz. each

2 tablespoons Marsala or sherry

2 tablespoons chopped fresh flatleaf parsley

a handful of arugula

salt and black pepper

rigatoni with *pork* and *lemon* ragu

2 tablespoons olive oil

14 oz. ground pork

1 onion, finely chopped

2 garlic cloves, crushed

4 anchovy fillets in oil, drained

2 tablespoons fresh rosemary needles

finely grated zest and juice of 1 unwaxed lemon

12 oz. dried pasta, such as rigatoni or penne

2 cups milk

⅔ cup pitted green olives, chopped

⅓ cup light cream

a good grating of fresh nutmeg

¼ cup Parmesan shavings, plus extra to serve

salt and black pepper

serves
4

M

In Italy, pork is often braised with milk, as it tenderizes the meat and the juices mingle with the milk to provide a sweet and meaty sauce. Rosemary is lovely and robust with pork but you could use chopped sage—just add it earlier when you brown the pork so it frazzles a little.

Put a large saucepan of salted water on to boil for the pasta.

Meanwhile, heat the olive oil in a large skillet over high heat and add the pork. Leave it for a few minutes until it browns, then turn it over and allow the other side to brown too. Add the onion, garlic, anchovies, rosemary, and lemon zest and stir to combine with the pork. Reduce the heat, cover, and let the onion soften for 10 minutes, stirring occasionally so the ingredients don't stick to the bottom of the skillet.

When the salted water in the large pan is boiling, add the pasta and cook according to the manufacturer's instructions until al dente.

When the onion is translucent, add the milk, lemon juice, and olives, and bring to a boil, uncovered, scraping the base of the skillet to loosen any sticky bits and incorporating them into the sauce. Simmer for about 15–20 minutes, or until about two-thirds of the liquid has evaporated and the pork is soft. Stir in the cream, then season with salt, pepper, and nutmeg.

Drain the rigatoni, put it back into its pan, and spoon in the pork ragu. Add the Parmesan shavings, stir well, and transfer to bowls. Sprinkle the extra Parmesan shavings on top.

lasagne

1 lb. dried lasagne sheets

1 quantity sauce from
the Spaghetti Bolognese
recipe (page 67)

10 oz. mozzarella, diced

¼ cup grated Parmesan

salt and black pepper

White sauce

4 cups milk

1 small garlic clove

4 tablespoons butter

⅓ cup all-purpose flour

*an ovenproof dish,
about 12 x 8 x 3 inches*

serves
8

M

Lasagne, just like Mom makes. It's a bit tricky and you'll need to be happy to spend some time in the kitchen, but just wait for the appreciative oohs and aahs round the table when you serve it up. Don't forget you need to have made the Bolognese sauce from the Spaghetti Bolognese recipe (page 67) first.

Preheat the oven to 375°F.

Bring a large saucepan of water to a boil. Add a pinch of salt, then the lasagne sheets, one at a time so that they don't stick together. Cook for 5 minutes, then drain and tip the lasagne into a bowl of cold water. Drain again and pat dry with paper towels.

To make the white sauce, put the milk and garlic into a small saucepan and heat gently until warm. Melt the butter in a separate saucepan, then stir in the flour and cook for 1 minute. Gradually add the warm milk, stirring constantly to make a smooth sauce. Bring to a boil, then simmer for 2–3 minutes. Remove and discard the garlic clove. Season with salt and pepper to taste.

Put 3–4 tablespoons of the Bolognese sauce into the ovenproof dish, spread evenly across the base of the dish, and cover with a layer of lasagne. Spoon over some white sauce and a few pieces of mozzarella and continue adding layers, starting with another layer of Bolognese sauce and finishing with the white sauce and mozzarella, until all the ingredients have been used. Sprinkle with pepper and Parmesan, then bake in the preheated oven for 30 minutes until the top is crusty and golden.

lasagne   carbonara

carbonara

This is not for the health-conscious: lots of eggs, cream, butter, Parmesan, and bacon. It's perennially popular, and for good reason. Make it for a special dinner and serve it with a leafy green salad to temper the richness of the pasta.

Bring a large saucepan of water to a boil. Add a good pinch of salt, then the pasta, and cook until al dente, or according to the manufacturer's instructions. Meanwhile, put the eggs and egg yolks in a bowl and mix lightly with a fork. Add the butter, cream, grated Parmesan, and lots of pepper. Let stand without mixing.

Chop the bacon into slivers. Cover the base of skillet with olive oil and heat through. When the oil is hot, add the bacon. When the fat starts to run from the bacon, add the garlic and stir well. Continue frying until the bacon becomes crisp and golden. Add the bacon and pan juices to the freshly cooked pasta and mix vigorously. Beat the egg mixture lightly with a fork and pour over the pasta. Mix well and serve at once with extra Parmesan and plenty of pepper—the butter will melt and the eggs will cook in the heat of the pasta.

serves 4–6

Q

M

1 lb. dried pasta, such as penne or spaghetti

Carbonara sauce

2 whole eggs

5 egg yolks

2 tablespoons butter

½ cup light cream

⅓ cup grated Parmesan, plus extra to serve

8 oz. bacon or prosciutto

olive oil, for frying

1 garlic clove, crushed

black pepper

sesame *chicken* and *vegetable* noodle salad

This recipe is typical of many with an Asian influence in that most of the sauce ingredients are pantry basics. That said, balsamic vinegar has replaced traditional Chinese black vinegar, which can be tricky to find. Similarly, if you're lucky enough to have a Chinese market near you, you will probably be able to find garlic chives but don't worry if not—just use regular chives instead. Unfortunately, watercress does perish quite quickly so try gently wrapping the leftovers in a clean, damp kitchen towel. Stored like this in the fridge, it should stay fresh for a couple of days.

Preheat the oven to 350°F.

To make the sesame dressing, put the sesame oil, soy sauce, vinegar, and sugar in a small bowl and stir for a few seconds until the sugar has dissolved. Set aside until needed.

Put the chicken in the roasting pan with ¼ cup water, cover firmly with aluminum foil, and cook in the preheated oven for 30 minutes. Remove from the oven and let cool. When cool enough to handle, shred the chicken and set aside.

Cook the noodles in boiling water for 3 minutes. Rinse them under cold water to cool and drain well. Heat the vegetable oil in a skillet over high heat. Add the chives, leeks, and bell pepper and stir-fry for 1 minute, until the vegetables have just softened. Remove the skillet from the heat and stir in the bean sprouts and watercress.

To serve, put the chicken, noodles, and vegetables in a large bowl. Add the dressing and sesame seeds and toss well.

serves
4

M

2 skinless chicken breast fillets

6 oz. thin egg noodles

2 tablespoons vegetable oil

2 handfuls of fresh garlic chives or regular chives, snipped into 1-inch lengths

1 leek, thinly sliced

1 small red bell pepper, seeded and thinly sliced

1 cup bean sprouts

a small bunch of watercress, leaves picked

1 tablespoon sesame seeds, lightly toasted in a dry skillet

Sesame dressing

2 tablespoons sesame oil

2 tablespoons light soy sauce

1 tablespoon balsamic vinegar

1 teaspoon sugar

a small roasting pan

vodka risotto with *lemon*

3 tablespoons olive oil

1 small onion, chopped

1 tender, inner celery stalk, chopped (optional)

3 garlic cloves, crushed

1⅓ cups risotto rice

about 6 cups hot vegetable stock

grated zest and juice of 1 unwaxed lemon

3 tablespoons vodka

2 tablespoons grated Parmesan, plus extra to serve

salt and black pepper

serves
4

V

Risotto is just the thing when friends drop in unexpectedly, and it's a very social dish to prepare if everyone helps with the stirring. It really only needs ingredients you're likely to have already, including vodka, a bottle of which is bound to be in the house somewhere. This recipe is light, so is especially good for impromptu late-night eating, but it is equally good as a side dish or appetizer since the flavors are subtle and go with most things. It can be made without celery, if you're improvising and have none, but everything else is mandatory.

Heat the oil in a large saucepan. Add the onion, celery (if using), and a pinch of salt. Cook over medium heat until soft, 2–3 minutes. Add the garlic and rice and continue cooking, stirring for about 1 minute, until the rice is well coated with oil.

Add a ladle of the stock and cook, stirring all the while, until the stock has been absorbed. Continue adding ladles of stock as the rice absorbs it. The rice is done when it is tender on the outside but still firm. Timing depends on the type and age of the rice, but 20–30 minutes is usual. Towards the end of cooking, add smaller ladles more often, rather than drowning the rice.

When the rice is cooked, stir in 1 tablespoon of the lemon zest, 2 tablespoons of the lemon juice, the vodka, Parmesan, and some pepper. Mix and taste for salt and lemon. Serve immediately with extra Parmesan and pepper.

*spaghetti and
arugula frittata*

spaghetti and *arugula* frittata

As with the frittata on page 145, this needs to be finished off under the broiler so make sure your skillet is ovenproof, and that the handle is away from the broiler's direct heat.

Heat 1 tablespoon of the oil in a saucepan, add the onion, and sauté for 5 minutes until softened. Add the garlic, tomatoes, and chile and cook for 3–4 minutes. Add the tomato paste and wine or water and simmer for 5 minutes. Remove from the heat, add the spaghetti, and toss gently.

Break the eggs into a large bowl and whisk briefly with a fork. Add the spaghetti and sauce and mix gently.

Heat the remaining oil in the skillet, add the spaghetti and egg mixture, and cook over low heat for 10–12 minutes, or until golden brown on the underside and almost set on the top. Meanwhile, preheat the broiler.

Sprinkle the frittata with the Parmesan and slide under the broiler for 30–60 seconds to melt the cheese and finish cooking the top. Let cool for 5 minutes, then transfer to a plate. Put the arugula on top, drizzle with balsamic vinegar, and serve immediately.

serves 4

V

3 tablespoons olive oil

1 onion, chopped

1 garlic clove, crushed

3 ripe tomatoes, chopped

1 fresh red chile, seeded and finely chopped

2 tablespoons tomato paste

⅔ cup white wine or water

2 cups cold cooked spaghetti (5 oz. before cooking)

6 extra-large eggs

2 tablespoons grated Parmesan

a small handful of arugula

2 tablespoons balsamic vinegar

salt and black pepper

a 12-inch nonstick skillet (measure the base, not the top)

prosciutto-wrapped *salmon* with *mashed potatoes*

This looks and tastes like food to impress, but it's effortless and has a very short shopping list.

Preheat the oven to 350°F.

Bring the potatoes to a boil in a pan of water, then simmer for 20 minutes, until soft. Drain and return to the pan, place over the heat, and shake to remove any excess moisture. Mash well, then mix in the egg and seasoning. Add the butter and mash again until creamy.

Meanwhile, season the salmon fillets and wrap in the prosciutto. Place on the prepared baking sheet and cook in the preheated oven for 15 minutes. Sprinkle with the dill and serve with the mashed potatoes.

serves 4

Q

F

2 lbs. potatoes, unpeeled and diced

1 egg

3 tablespoons butter

4 salmon fillets, about 4 oz. each, skinned and boned

4 slices of prosciutto

a bunch of fresh dill, chopped

salt and black pepper

a baking sheet, lightly greased

fish baked with *lemon,* oregano, and *potatoes*

serves
4

F

½ cup olive oil

2 onions, thinly sliced

2 garlic cloves, crushed

1–2 pinches of hot red pepper flakes

1 teaspoon crushed coriander seeds

½ teaspoon dried oregano, plus extra to serve

1½ lbs. potatoes, cut into wedges

2 dried bay leaves

¼ cup white wine

½ teaspoon grated lemon zest

1½ lbs. any firm white fish, skinned, boned, and cut into large chunks

2 small lemons, halved

1 tablespoon chopped fresh flatleaf parsley

salt and black pepper

a large ovenproof dish

If you have a stovetop-to-oven pan, this dish can be cooked in one pot. Use chunks of firm white fish such as cod, haddock, hake, or monkfish and choose potatoes that don't break up on cooking—large, waxy salad potatoes are ideal. As a rule of thumb, yellow-fleshed potatoes are waxy, while white potatoes tend to be floury. Some steamed greens tossed in a little olive oil make a great accompaniment to this dish.

Heat a large regular skillet or ovenproof lidded skillet over medium heat and add the oil. Add the onion and fry for 2–3 minutes, then turn the heat down low. Add 1–2 pinches of salt, cover, and let the onion cook very gently for 10–12 minutes until soft and golden yellow. Add the garlic, red pepper flakes, crushed coriander seeds, and oregano. Cook for another 3–4 minutes.

Add the potatoes and bay leaves to the skillet, turning them in the oily onions. Season with 1 teaspoon salt and several turns of the pepper mill, cook for a few minutes, then add the wine and lemon zest. When it bubbles, cover and cook gently for 15–20 minutes or until the potatoes are just tender. Meanwhile, preheat the oven to 400°F.

Transfer the potatoes to the ovenproof dish, if necessary. Season the fish with a little salt, then nestle the fish into the potatoes. Squeeze a little lemon juice from one of the lemon halves over the fish and spoon over a little of the oily juices. Add the lemon halves to the dish and turn in the oil.

Bake, uncovered, in the preheated oven for 20–25 minutes, basting once or twice, until the potatoes are fully tender and the fish cooked through. The lemons should be touched with brown. Serve immediately, sprinkled with more oregano and the parsley.

flaked *haddock* moussaka

This is one of those meals that is extremely comforting in the winter served with mashed potatoes, and yet works equally well in the summer alongside a large green salad.

Preheat the oven to 375°F.

Check the haddock for any remaining bones and discard them. Put the fish in the prepared ovenproof dish and sprinkle with the lemon juice.

Cook the zucchini for just 1 minute in boiling water, then drain, pat dry, and place on top of the fish.

Beat the egg and cream together, add the nutmeg and dill, and pour over the fish and zucchini. Sprinkle over the grated Cheddar, then put the dish in a small roasting pan half filled with cold water. Bake in the preheated oven for 45 minutes, or until the top is golden brown.

serves 4

F

12 oz. haddock fillets, skinned and diced

1 teaspoon lemon juice

4 zucchini, thinly sliced

2 eggs

1¼ cups light cream

a pinch of freshly grated nutmeg

a little fresh dill, finely chopped

½ cup grated Cheddar

a shallow ovenproof dish, greased

a small roasting pan

stir-fried *seafood* with *bell peppers* and *leeks*

Keeping a bag of mixed seafood in the freezer is a great standby for a fast meal. It can be added frozen to rice dishes, pasta, or soup—just make sure it is cooked for a few minutes longer than fresh seafood, until piping hot.

Heat 1 tablespoon of the oil in a large skillet. Add the bell peppers, leeks, and onion and stir-fry over high heat until lightly brown. Add the cherry tomatoes and cook for a further 2 minutes. Remove the vegetables from the skillet and set aside in a warm place until needed.

Heat the remaining oil in the same skillet. Add the garlic, red pepper flakes, and mixed seafood and stir-fry over high heat. Cook for 3–4 minutes, stirring occasionally (or cook for 7–8 minutes if the seafood is frozen).

Mix the warm vegetables with the seafood and add the balsamic vinegar and cilantro at the last moment. Serve immediately.

serves 2

Q

F

2 tablespoons olive oil

1 red bell pepper, seeded and cut into thin strips

2 leeks, cut into strips

1 large onion, cut into thick wedges

5 oz. cherry tomatoes, halved

2 garlic cloves, crushed

1 teaspoon hot red pepper flakes

10 oz. frozen mixed seafood, such as shrimp, mussels, scallops, and squid rings, either defrosted or frozen

chopped cilantro, to serve

2 teaspoons balsamic vinegar

1 lb. 4 oz. pork fillet, cut into
1-inch chunks

1 tablespoon light soy sauce

2 teaspoons finely grated
fresh ginger

2 tablespoons vegetable oil

1 large red bell pepper,
seeded and cut into
1-inch chunks

1 large onion, cut into
8 wedges

½ large cucumber, roughly
peeled, halved, seeded,
and thickly sliced

10 oz. canned pineapple, cut
into 1-inch chunks

Sauce

⅓ cup pineapple juice

¼ cup tomato ketchup

2 tablespoons rice vinegar

1 tablespoon light soy sauce

1 tablespoon sugar

1 tablespoon cornstarch

sweet and sour *pork* with *pineapple* and *cucumber*

serves
4

M

A world away from the local takeout's greasy battered nuggets
drowned in a fluorescent gloop, this scrumptious recipe uses
lean pork fillet fried with cucumber wedges and juicy pineapple
chunks and lightly coated in a sweet and tangy sauce. Serve it
with your favorite accompaniment—rice, noodles, or a pita or
other flat bread to mop up the juices.

Combine all the sauce ingredients in a bowl and set aside.

Put the pork, soy sauce, and ginger in a bowl and mix well. Cover and
marinate in the refrigerator for 20 minutes, if possible.

Heat the oil in a large skillet until hot, then add the pork in batches
(don't over-crowd the skillet, otherwise the pork will stew rather than fry).
Stir-fry over high heat for 4–5 minutes until nearly cooked through and
well sealed all over. Remove the pork from the skillet and set aside.

Throw the bell pepper and onion into the skillet and stir-fry for 2–3 minutes.
Return the pork to the skillet with any juices. Pour in the sauce and toss
everything together. Bring to a boil, then reduce the heat. Add the cucumber
and pineapple and simmer gently for 3–4 minutes, or until the sauce has
thickened and the pork is cooked through. Serve with the accompaniment
of your choice.

quiche lorraine

Ready-made shortcrust pastry is available in supermarkets. It comes ready rolled or in a block. You'll need to weigh down the pastry when you bake it blind and for this you can use special ceramic baking beans, rice, dried beans, or pasta.

serves
4–6

M

14 oz. storebought shortcrust pastry

7 oz. chopped bacon or cubed pancetta

5 eggs, plus 1 extra, lightly beaten with a fork, to glaze

¾ cup heavy cream or crème fraîche

freshly grated nutmeg, to taste

½ cup grated Gruyère

salt and black pepper

a tart pan, 9 inches in diameter

baking beans, rice, dried beans, or pasta, for blind baking

a baking sheet

Preheat the oven to 400°F.

Roll out the pastry thinly on a lightly floured work surface until it is slightly bigger than the tart pan. Lay the pastry carefully over the pan and press it into shape all around the edges. Cut away any excess pastry with a knife. Prick the base all over with a fork, then chill or freeze for 15 minutes to set the pastry.

Line the base with aluminum foil and fill with baking beans or whatever you have chosen. Set on the baking sheet and bake blind in the center of the preheated oven for about 10–12 minutes. Remove the foil and baking beans and return the pastry crust to the oven for a further 5–7 minutes to dry out completely. To prevent the pastry from becoming soggy, brush the blind-baked crust with the beaten egg—you can do this when it is hot or cold. Bake again for 5–10 minutes until set and shiny. This will also fill and seal any holes made when pricking before the blind baking.

Heat a nonstick skillet and fry the bacon or pancetta until brown and crisp, then drain on paper towels. Scatter over the base of the pastry crust.

Put the eggs and cream into a bowl, beat well, and season with salt, pepper, and nutmeg to taste. Carefully pour the mixture over the bacon and sprinkle with the Gruyère.

Bake for about 25 minutes until just set, golden brown, and puffy. Serve warm or at room temperature.

sausage, sun-dried tomato, and *potato* tart

serves **4–6**

M

1 lb. storebought shortcrust pastry

1 egg, lightly beaten with a fork, to glaze

Sausage and onion filling

12 oz. sausages

3 tablespoons olive oil

3 onions, thinly sliced

2 garlic cloves, crushed

8 oz. potatoes, chopped

1 tablespoon all-purpose flour

2–3 tablespoons tomato paste

12 sun-dried tomato halves in oil, chopped

1 teaspoon hot red pepper flakes

2 teaspoons dried Herbes de Provence

⅔ cup mascarpone

salt and black pepper

a tart pan, 9 inches in diameter and 1½ inches deep

baking beans, rice, dried beans, or pasta, for blind baking

a baking sheet

There is a fabulous blend of flavors in this tart. The mascarpone is dotted onto the sausage mixture before the onions are piled on top—so it just melts in.

Bring the pastry to room temperature. Meanwhile, preheat the oven to 400°F.

Roll out the pastry thinly on a lightly floured work surface until it is slightly bigger than the tart pan. Lay the pastry carefully over the pan and press it into shape all around the edges. Cut away any excess pastry with a knife. Prick the base all over with a fork, then chill or freeze for 15 minutes to set the pastry.

Line the base with aluminum foil and fill with baking beans or whatever you have chosen. Set on the baking sheet and bake blind in the center of the preheated oven for about 10–12 minutes. Remove the foil and baking beans and return the pastry crust to the oven for a further 5–7 minutes to dry out completely. To prevent the pastry from becoming soggy, brush the blind-baked crust with the beaten egg—you can do this when it is hot or cold. Bake again for 5–10 minutes until set and shiny. This will also fill and seal any holes made when pricking before the blind baking.

To make the sausage and onion filling, cut away the skins of the sausages and pull the sausage meat into chunks. Heat the oil in a large saucepan, add the onions, garlic, and 3 tablespoons water. Cover and cook over gentle heat for about 1 hour or until meltingly soft but not colored. Stir the onions occasionally and watch for catching. Let the onions cool.

Blanch the potatoes in boiling salted water for 1 minute, then drain and set aside. Heat a nonstick skillet and add the sausage meat, breaking it up with a wooden spoon as it cooks and browns. After about 5 minutes, stir in the flour, tomato paste, sun-dried tomatoes, red pepper flakes, herbs, and salt and pepper to taste. Cook for another 5 minutes, then stir in the potatoes. Spoon this into the pastry crust and dot small spoonfuls of the mascarpone over the surface. Cover with a layer of the cooked onions, then bake for 25 minutes until the onions are golden.

cumin-spiced
lamb chops

roast *potatoes, chorizo,* and *lemon*

Simple roast potatoes are endlessly popular, but sometimes it's fun to jazz them up with extra flavor.

Preheat the oven to 400°F Gas 6.

Cut the potatoes into large pieces. Put in a large saucepan and cover with water. Bring to a boil and boil for 5 minutes. Drain in a colander and let dry out for 5 minutes. Toss the potatoes around in the colander to rough up the outsides.

Pour the oil into the roasting pan. Heat in the preheated oven for 5 minutes. Add the potatoes and garlic to the hot oil with plenty of salt and stir well to coat. Roast for 20 minutes, then remove the pan from the oven, stir again, and add the chorizo, lemon, and rosemary. Return to the hot oven and continue roasting for a further 20 minutes. Serve immediately.

2 lbs. potatoes

3 whole garlic bulbs, cut in half crosswise

3 tablespoons olive oil

3 small chorizo sausages, diagonally sliced

1 lemon, halved lengthwise and sliced

2 tablespoons fresh rosemary needles

salt

a large roasting pan

cumin-spiced *lamb* chops

Here are some lemony, minty broiled lamb chops accompanied by ultra-easy chickpea mash made with canned chickpeas.

To make the marinade, combine the olive oil, mint, lemon zest and 1 tablespoon of the juice, the ground chiles, and garlic in a large bowl. Add the lamb chops, season well with salt and pepper, and toss. If you have time, marinate for an hour; if not, move swiftly on.

Heat ½ tablespoon of the olive oil in a skillet, add the cumin seeds, and stir for 30 seconds until fragrant. Tip in the chickpeas and toss in the oil for 1 minute. Stir in the remaining lemon juice and ⅓ cup water, cover, and simmer for 10 minutes until softened. Meanwhile, preheat the broiler to high.

Put the lamb chops on the prepared baking sheet and broil for 5–6 minutes until blackened around the edges. Turn over, add the tomatoes, drizzle with the remaining olive oil, season, and broil for 5–6 minutes.

Mash the chickpeas with a potato masher until you get a chunky purée. Add the cilantro, season to taste, and stir. Transfer to bowls and top with 3 lamb chops. Drizzle with the lamb juices.

12 medium lamb chops

2 tablespoons olive oil

1 teaspoon cumin seeds

2 x 14-oz cans chickpeas, drained

10 oz. cherry tomatoes

¼ cup chopped cilantro

salt and black pepper

Marinade

2 tablespoons olive oil

2 tablespoons chopped fresh mint

finely grated zest of 1 unwaxed lemon, plus 5 tablespoons juice

1 teaspoon ground chiles

1 garlic clove, crushed

a baking sheet, lined with aluminum foil

*ground beef
and pea curry*

*beef
rendang*

ground beef and *pea* curry

serves 4

M

Ground beef is cooked slowly with spices and peas resulting in a subtle, fragrant curry, which is great when accompanied by either Spiced Eggplant Dahl (page 145), steamed basmati rice, or naan bread—or all of the above!

Heat the oil in a large, heavy-based saucepan and add the onion. Cook over low heat for 15–20 minutes, until softened and just turning light golden. Add the garlic, ginger, chiles, cumin seeds, and curry paste and stir-fry over high heat for 1–2 minutes.

Add the ground beef and stir-fry for 3–4 minutes, then stir in the canned tomatoes, sugar, and tomato paste and bring to a boil. Season well, cover, and reduce the heat to low. Cook for 1–1½ hours. 10 minutes before the end of the cooking time, add the coconut cream and peas.

To serve, garnish with the cilantro and serve with accompaniments of your choice.

2 tablespoons safflower oil

1 large onion, finely chopped

3 garlic cloves, crushed

1 teaspoon finely grated fresh ginger

3–4 green chiles (seeded if desired), thinly sliced

1 tablespoon cumin seeds

3 tablespoons medium curry paste

1 lb. 12 oz. ground beef

14-oz. can chopped tomatoes

1 teaspoon sugar

¼ cup tomato paste

¼ cup coconut cream

1½ cups frozen peas

salt and black pepper

a large handful of cilantro, chopped, to garnish

beef rendang

This is a gentle, aromatic meat curry from Indonesia made all in one pot, with cubes of beef. Tamarind paste is sold in small jars from supermarkets or Asian stores. Like all the best curries, this one needs to cook slowly and gently on the stove so that the meat has time to tenderize and absorb the flavors from the spices. Serve it with Thai jasmine rice and green beans.

serves
4

M

1 lb. steak for stewing

1 tablespoon tamarind paste

1 cinnamon stick

1 tablespoon brown sugar

2 tablespoons soy sauce

1 cup hot beef or vegetable stock

¼ teaspoon ground black pepper

¼ teaspoon freshly grated nutmeg

6 green cardamom pods

2 red onions, very finely chopped

3 garlic cloves, crushed

1-inch piece of fresh ginger, peeled and finely chopped

Put the meat in a heavy medium saucepan or casserole dish. Add the tamarind, cinnamon stick, sugar, soy sauce, stock, pepper, and nutmeg.

Crush the cardamom pods with a mortar and pestle (or with the end of a rolling pin). Throw away the green husks and keep the tiny black seeds. Crush the seeds and add to the pan with the onions, garlic, and ginger. Stir until well mixed.

Set the pan over medium heat and bring the mixture to a boil. Stir, then cover the pan with a lid and turn down the heat to very low so the mixture bubbles very gently.

Let cook for 1½ hours, stirring now and then.

Finally, remove the lid and cook uncovered for 20–30 minutes until the sauce is very thick. Remove the cinnamon stick and serve.

steak with *new potatoes, roquefort,* and *arugula*

1½ lbs. new potatoes

4 x 8-oz. sirloin or rib-eye steaks (1 inch thick)

⅓ cup olive oil

1 garlic clove, crushed

2 tablespoons capers

finely grated zest and juice of 1 unwaxed lemon

a handful of arugula

2½ oz. Roquefort

salt and black pepper

a ridged grill pan (optional)

serves 4

M

Cooking steaks well is all about getting the pan very hot and creating a golden crust on the meat which prevents any juices from escaping. Let them rest after cooking and squeeze over lemon juice (an Italian trick), which cuts through the richness of the meat. When finishing the potatoes, don't be stingy with the olive oil: use a liberal amount of good-quality oil as it's not being cooked so you really taste the flavors.

Put a medium saucepan of water on to boil. Add a large pinch of salt and the potatoes. Simmer gently for 20–22 minutes until very tender, then drain and return to the pan.

Meanwhile, heat the grill pan or a large skillet over very high heat. Drizzle the steaks with 1 tablespoon of the olive oil and season. When the pan is smoking, add the steaks. Let them cook, without turning them over, for 3 minutes. Now turn them over and cook for a further 2–3 minutes. Prod them to check if they are done to your liking: a little give means medium and lots of give means rare. Transfer them to a plate, cover with aluminum foil, and let rest for a few minutes.

Mix the remaining olive oil with the garlic, capers, and lemon zest in a small measuring jug, season well, and set aside. Lightly crush the potatoes with the back of a spoon until they buckle a little, then fold in the arugula and olive oil. Crumble over the Roquefort cheese and transfer to bowls. Pour the lemon juice all over the steaks and cut into strips. Lift onto the potatoes, pour over any steak juices, and grind over some pepper.

beef fajitas with *guacamole* and *sour cream*

Since your friends can help themselves and put together their own traditional fajitas, this dish is terrifically straightforward to serve. If you like a very spicy guacamole, add a couple of extra jalapeño chiles, seeded and finely chopped.

serves
4–6

M

Preheat the oven to 325°F.

Remove any fat from the beef and cut it diagonally, across the grain, to create finger-length strips. Mix together 2 tablespoons of oil, the pimentón, and cumin in a large bowl. Add the beef pieces and toss until evenly coated in the spiced oil. Set aside.

Heat a large skillet over high heat with the remaining oil and stir-fry the red onion, bell pepper, and garlic for 3–4 minutes, until they start to go limp and the edges begin to blacken. Remove from the skillet and set aside in a warm place.

Wrap the tortillas in aluminum foil and place them in the preheated oven to warm for about 5 minutes. (Alternatively, you can follow the manufacturer's instructions for warming them in a microwave.)

Meanwhile, wipe the skillet clean with paper towels. Heat until smoking hot, then drop the strips of meat into the skillet over high heat, working in batches and turning them frequently. Each batch should take no more than 1–2 minutes to cook. Season the meat with salt and pepper.

To serve, arrange the beef strips, guacamole, bell peppers, onion, jalapeño chiles, arugula, sour cream, and hot chili sauce, if using, in separate bowls. Wrap the tortillas in a cloth napkin and put them in a basket or dish (so that they don't dry out and go hard) and bring them to the table. Let everyone dig in.

4 x 6-oz. sirloin steaks
(1 inch thick)

¼ cup olive oil

1 tablespoon pimentón
(Spanish oak-smoked
paprika)

1 tablespoon ground cumin

1 large red onion, cut
into petals

1 red or green bell pepper,
seeded and thinly sliced

3 garlic cloves, thinly sliced

8–12 soft wheat or cornstarch
tortillas

salt and black pepper

To serve

Guacamole (page 19)

2–3 jalapeño chiles, seeded
and chopped

a handful of arugula

hot chili sauce (optional)

sour cream

lemony poached *chicken*

2 small, unwaxed lemons, each cut into 6 wedges

a 5-lb. chicken

2 tablespoons olive oil

1 whole garlic bulb, cloves separated but left unpeeled

a small bunch of fresh sage

4 cups milk

salt and black pepper

bread, to serve

This recipe is for a whole chicken. After an hour on the stove, the chicken is juicy and the sauce is sticky and lemony.

Season the chicken all over with salt and pepper. Heat half the olive oil in a large saucepan and cook the chicken, breast-side down, for 4–5 minutes, until golden. Turn the chicken over and cook for 3–4 minutes more. Remove the chicken from the pan and pour away any used oil. Pour the remaining olive oil into the pan and add the lemon wedges and garlic. Stir-fry for 2–3 minutes, until golden. Add the sage and cook for another minute or so.

Return the chicken to the pan and pour the milk over it. Put a lid on the pan, leaving a little opening to allow the steam to escape. Simmer over gentle heat for about 1 hour, until the meat is cooked through and the sauce has curdled into sticky nuggets (keep the heat low, or the milk will reduce too quickly to cook the chicken). Remove the pan from the heat. Let rest for 4–5 minutes before slicing. Serve warm with chunks of bread to mop up the sauce. Squeeze the softened garlic out and spread onto the bread.

hamburgers

1 lb. 4 oz. ground beef

1 garlic clove, crushed

1 shallot, finely diced

a bunch of fresh parsley, chopped

1 tablespoon olive oil

1 teaspoon Worcestershire sauce

4 slices of bacon

4 individual ciabatta loaves

¼ cup mayonnaise

4 slices of beef tomato

1 cup grated Cheddar

1 avocado, sliced

shredded iceberg lettuce

salt and black pepper

Burgers are fantastically versatile, so build yours just as you like, with or without the suggested garnishes.

Preheat the broiler.

Put the beef, garlic, shallot, parsley, and Worcestershire sauce in a large bowl, season with salt and pepper, and mix well with your hands. Divide the mixture into 4 and shape into burgers.

Heat some oil in a large skillet and cook for 2 minutes on each side for rare, 3 minutes for medium-rare, and 4 minutes for well done.

Meanwhile, broil the bacon until crisp. Cut the ciabatta loaves in half and broil the insides. Spread the insides with mayonnaise. Put a slice of tomato on the broiled base and a burger on top, followed by a handful of cheese, a bacon slice, a slice or two of avocado, and some lettuce. Sandwich together with the remaining bread and serve with ketchup and mustard.

italian *roast chicken*

This is a dead easy Sunday lunch and there's no excuse not to give it a try: the smell of roasting chicken is, after all, irresistible, plus, because this dish uses chicken pieces, there's no difficult carving, and the gravy magically appears during cooking. Choose chicken legs if you're hungry, otherwise large thighs, because these have the most flavor. Serve with Roasties (page 195) or pasta and a green vegetable or a leafy salad.

Preheat the oven to 425°F.

Put the chicken pieces into the ovenproof dishes, skin side up, and check that the pieces don't overlap each other. Put the garlic cloves in the dishes between the chicken pieces. Pour the lemon juice all over the chicken, then pour the oil over the top so the skin is evenly coated in liquid. Sprinkle with 4 pinches of salt and then about 3 turns of the pepper grinder. Finally, set a sprig of thyme or rosemary on the top of each piece of chicken.

Put the chicken in the preheated oven. Roast for 40 minutes for large legs, and 35 minutes for thighs. As the chicken cooks, the legs become a crispy golden brown, surrounded by a light brown cooking-juice gravy. Make sure the juices run clear and the meat is fully cooked before removing from the oven. Serve with Roasties and gravy from the dishes.

serves
4

M

4 chicken legs or thighs

4 garlic cloves, unpeeled

juice of 1 large lemon

2 tablespoons olive oil

4 large sprigs of fresh thyme or rosemary

salt and black pepper

1 or 2 ovenproof dishes, big enough to hold the chicken in one layer

2 tablespoons olive oil

4 lbs. chicken pieces, such as legs, thighs, and wings

8 garlic cloves, thinly sliced

14-oz. can chopped tomatoes

a pinch of sugar

2 oz. pitted black olives, roughly chopped

salt and black pepper

a bunch of fresh basil, torn

chicken with *tomato, garlic,* and *olives*

serves
4–6

M

Here's another effortless option for cooking a large quantity of chicken to feed hungry, appreciative friends, but it's cooked on the stove rather than roasted. It goes well with rice or pasta.

Heat 1 tablespoon of the oil in a large saucepan. Add the chicken pieces and brown on all sides. Transfer the chicken to a plate, salt generously, and set aside. Add the remaining oil and garlic and cook for 1 minute, then add the tomatoes and sugar. Stir well and return the chicken to the pan. Cover and simmer gently until the chicken is cooked, 25–30 minutes. Transfer to a serving dish, then raise the heat and cook the sauce to thicken slightly, about 10 minutes. Add salt and pepper to taste, then stir in the olives. Pour the sauce over the chicken and sprinkle with the basil.

1¾ lbs. boneless, skinless chicken thighs, cut into bite-size pieces

1 lb. frozen spinach, thawed

2 tablespoons safflower oil

1 onion, finely chopped

2 teaspoons cumin seeds

⅔ cup hot chicken stock

1 tablespoon lemon juice

salt and black pepper

Marinade

½ cup plain yogurt (not low-fat)

2 tablespoons crushed garlic

2 tablespoons finely grated fresh ginger

2 tablespoons ground coriander

2 tablespoons medium curry powder

chicken and *spinach* curry

serves
4

M

This is a velvety curry which needs some forward planning as the chicken has to marinate for 3–4 hours or overnight.

To make the marinade, combine the yogurt, garlic, ginger, coriander, and curry powder in a large glass bowl and season well. Stir in the chicken, cover, and refrigerate for 3–4 hours or overnight.

Put the spinach in a saucepan and cook for 8–10 minutes. Drain thoroughly, then chop as finely as possible. Season well with salt and pepper.

Heat the oil in a large, nonstick skillet and add the onion. Cook over gentle heat for 10–12 minutes. Add the cumin seeds and stir-fry for 1–2 minutes. Increase the heat to high and add the marinated chicken (discarding the marinade). Stir-fry for 6–8 minutes. Pour in the stock and spinach and bring to a boil. Reduce the heat to low, cover tightly, and cook for 25–30 minutes, or until the chicken is cooked through.

Uncover the skillet, check the seasoning, and cook over high heat for 3–4 minutes, stirring often. Remove from the heat and stir in the lemon.

chicken with tomato,
garlic, and olives

roast chicken with garlic, apple, and cider

This is the roast to choose when there are just two of you and it's a bit of a special occasion. Don't be alarmed by the amount of garlic that goes into the dish—the flavor becomes much more subtle once the garlic is blanched. Serve with broccoli and new potatoes.

Preheat the oven to 400°F.

Bring a small pan of water to a boil and cook the garlic cloves for 2–3 minutes, or until tender. Drain and set aside until needed.

Season the chicken breasts and drizzle with the olive oil. Put them on the baking sheet and place on the top shelf of the preheated oven to cook for about 25 minutes, or until the chicken is cooked through and the skin is golden.

Meanwhile, put the garlic, cider, chopped apple, and mustard in a large skillet. Cook gently over low heat for about 10 minutes.

When the chicken is cooked, remove it from the oven and transfer to the skillet. Add the cream or crème fraîche to the skillet and simmer for 5 minutes. Use the back of a fork to squash the garlic down into the sauce, taking care not to squash the apples too. Season with salt and pepper to taste. Stir in the parsley and serve immediately, with broccoli spears and new potatoes.

Variation This classic French sauce also tastes really good served with oven-roasted or broiled pork chops.

serves
2

M

4 garlic cloves, peeled but left whole

2 skinless chicken breast fillets

2 tablespoons olive oil

½ cup hard apple cider

1 red apple, peeled, cored, and diced

2 tablespoons Dijon mustard

¼ cup heavy cream or crème fraîche

a handful of chopped fresh parsley

salt and black pepper

broccoli spears and new potatoes, to serve

a baking sheet

tarragon chicken casserole

serves 4

M

4 skinless and boneless chicken thighs, diced

2 large leeks, cut into chunks

2 garlic cloves, crushed

⅔ cup hot chicken stock

grated zest and juice of ½ unwaxed lemon

1 teaspoon dried tarragon

14-oz. can navy beans, drained and rinsed

6½ oz. thin green beans

2 tablespoons sour cream

salt and black pepper

A good casserole is hard to beat, especially on a cold winter's evening. It tends to taste even better the following day so treat yourself to the leftovers with some crusty bread.

Season the chicken with salt and pepper and dry-fry in a nonstick skillet for 3 minutes until browned. Transfer to a casserole dish or large saucepan. Add the leeks and garlic to the skillet with 2 tablespoons of the stock and cook for 2 minutes, then tip into the casserole dish.

Pour the remaining stock into the casserole dish and add the lemon zest and juice, tarragon, and navy beans. Bring to a simmer, cover, and cook gently for 15 minutes.

Stir in the green beans, re-cover, and cook for a further 15 minutes until the beans are tender but still have some bite. Finally, stir in the sour cream just before serving.

roasted vegetable dauphinois

serves 4

V

1 garlic clove, peeled but left whole

melted butter, for brushing

1 lb. parsnips, cut into ½-inch diagonal slices

a handful of fresh sage leaves

12 oz. carrots, cut into ½-inch diagonal slices

12 oz. uncooked beetroot, scrubbed well and cut into ½-inch diagonal slices

1¼ cups heavy cream

1 tablespoon olive oil

salt and black pepper

an ovenproof dish

This rich, creamy, garlicky sauce is offset by the earthy flavors of root vegetables. It is incredibly straightforward to make and it's delicious served with lamb or beef.

Preheat the oven to 400°F.

Rub the garlic around the base and sides of the ovenproof dish, then brush with melted butter. Pack overlapping slices of parsnips into the dish. Season well with salt and pepper, then add one-third of the sage leaves. Repeat the process, first with the carrots, then the beetroot, seasoning each layer with salt and pepper and dotting with the remaining sage. Pour in the cream.

Cover the dish with aluminum foil and bake in the preheated oven for 1 hour 40 minutes. Remove the foil and lightly sprinkle the top with the olive oil. Return to the oven and continue cooking for a further 20 minutes or until the vegetables are very tender.

roasted vegetable dauphinois

roasties

roasties

It's hard to imagine a roast dinner without crunchy roast potatoes, not to mention roast parsnips, roast sweet potatoes, and more. So here is an easy way to cook all your favorite vegetables in one roasting pan.

Preheat the oven to 425°F.

Put all the vegetables in the roasting pan. Pour the oil over the top, sprinkle with the salt and pepper, then add the herbs, pushing them between the vegetables. Using both hands, toss the vegetables in the oil and seasonings so they are very well mixed. Spread out the vegetables so they are in a single layer.

Bake in the preheated oven for about 1 hour, but every 15 minutes during the cooking time, remove the pan carefully from the oven and gently turn over the vegetables so they cook and brown evenly.

At the end of the cooking time, transfer the roasties to a serving dish, removing any large sprigs of thyme or rosemary.

1 lb. baking potatoes, cut into chunks

1 lb. parsnips, cut into chunks

1 lb. sweet potatoes, cut into chunks

1 lb. large carrots, cut into chunks

3 tablespoons olive oil

salt and black pepper

3 sprigs of fresh thyme or rosemary (or both)

a large roasting pan

potatoes boulangère

Finely sliced potatoes cooked in a stock and allowed to dry and crisp on top: edible heaven.

Preheat the oven to 350°F.

Put a layer of potatoes in the buttered dish, then add a layer of onions. Season well with salt and pepper, then repeat the layers until all the ingredients are used. Finish with a neat layer of potatoes overlapping each other and push down firmly.

Pour on the hot stock and dot the top with the butter. Bake in the preheated oven for about 1½ hours or until the top is golden brown and crunchy and the potatoes are soft right through when tested with the point of a knife.

2 lbs. floury potatoes, sliced

2 onions, finely sliced

1¼ cups hot vegetable stock

2 tablespoons butter, finely diced

salt and black pepper

a 9-inch shallow, ovenproof dish, greased

sweet things

french *pancakes*

¾ cup all-purpose flour

1 extra-large egg

1¼ cups milk

a little butter or
vegetable oil, for frying

It's great fun (and less work for you) to set up a "pancake bar" on the kitchen table and let everyone help themselves to their favorite topping (see below).

Put the flour in a large bowl and make a hollow in the middle. Crack the egg into the hollow and start to whisk it in with a balloon whisk. Gradually pour in the milk and continue to whisk until the batter is well mixed and smooth. Cover and chill for 30 minutes. (The batter can be made in advance and kept for up to 24 hours.)

Wipe a skillet with the butter and heat. Add a ladleful of batter, tilting the skillet to spread it evenly. Cook for 1–2 minutes on each side until light brown. Stack the pancakes on a large plate and keep warm.

pancake toppings

The simplest ideas are often the best, so here are some quick and easy toppings.

Quick chocolate sauce

5 oz. bittersweet chocolate

2 tablespoons corn syrup

5 tablespoons unsalted butter

1 tablespoon brandy (optional)

Put all the ingredients in a small saucepan and melt over low heat, stirring continuously until smooth.

Lemon and sugar

The classic way of serving pancakes: squeeze some lemon juice over the top and sprinkle with a little sugar.

Honey and walnuts

Offer a pot of honey with a drizzler and a little dish of chopped walnuts for scattering.

Fruit jam and cream

Spread raspberry or strawberry jam on the pancake and top generously with crème fraîche or sour cream.

muffin mania

Use this basic recipe to create different kinds of flavored muffins. If you prepare the dry mix the day before, you can quickly rustle up some freshly-baked muffins in the morning.

Preheat the oven to 350°F.

Sift the flour, sugar, baking powder, and salt together into a large bowl or plastic bag.

Whisk the egg in a large bowl with a balloon whisk, then whisk in the milk and oil. Add the dry ingredients and stir with a wooden spoon until just blended. The mixture should look very coarse with lumps and floury pockets. This will make the muffins light and fluffy when they're baked.

Spoon into the cases in the muffin pan, filling them three-quarters full. Bake in the preheated oven for about 20 minutes or until well risen and golden brown.

Remove from the oven and leave for a couple of minutes, then pop the muffins out of the pan. Serve warm—they do not reheat well.

Variations

• Experiment with different flours, and adjust the liquid accordingly because whole-wheat flours tend to absorb more liquid.
• Add nuts, seeds, and dried fruits to the basic mixture.
• Use brown sugar instead of granulated sugar.
• Sift in spices with the dry ingredients.
• Quickly stir whole berries or chopped fresh fruit into the mix before baking.
• For a crunchy topping, mix chopped nuts and seeds into brown sugar and sprinkle on top of the muffins before baking.

1⅓ cups all-purpose flour

⅔ cup granulated sugar

1 tablespoon baking powder

½ teaspoon salt

1 extra-large egg

½ cup milk (or a little more)

¼ cup safflower oil

a 6- or 12-cup muffin pan, lined with paper cases

double *chocolate* muffins

makes
12

V

Everybody loves chocolate muffins! These are very quick to whip up and made with cocoa powder plus chocolate chips for maximum chocolate flavor. The brilliant thing about muffins is how versatile they are, and how popular. Bake a batch and take them round to a friend who is feeling blue, make a large number for hungry revellers at a house party, or keep a few in the freezer for days when you crave a chocolatey treat.

Preheat the oven to 400°F.

Sift the flour, cocoa powder, sugar, and baking powder together into a large bowl or plastic bag. Add the chocolate chips.

Whisk the eggs in a large bowl with a balloon whisk, then whisk in the milk, oil, and vanilla. Add the dry ingredients and stir with a wooden spoon until just blended. The mixture should look very coarse with lumps and floury pockets. This will make the muffins light and fluffy when they're baked.

Spoon into the cases in the muffin pan, filling them about half full. Dot the chocolate chips over the top. Bake in the preheated oven for about 20 minutes or until well risen and just firm. The chocolate chips become very hot, so take care not to touch them.

Remove from the oven and leave for a couple of minutes, then pop the muffins out of the pan. Serve warm—they do not reheat well.

1¾ cups all-purpose flour

½ cup cocoa powder

½ cup sugar

2 teaspoons baking powder

2 tablespoons chocolate chips, plus extra for sprinkling

2 extra-large eggs

1 cup milk

½ cup safflower oil

1 teaspoon pure vanilla extract

a 12-cup deep muffin pan, lined with paper cases

cheat's cherry
brûlée

cheat's *cherry* brûlée

Real crème brûlée is creamy, indulgent, and a bit tricky to make. This is the cheat's alternative. Don't be put off by needing to buy both light cream and cream cheese—you can use up the light cream in the Nutty Chocolate and Marshmallow Toast on page 199 and the cream cheese for your sandwiches.

Preheat the broiler.

Put the cherries in a saucepan with ½ cup water. Cook over high heat until simmering, then lower the heat and simmer gently until the fruit has slightly softened, 5–7 minutes. Remove the pan from the heat.

Put the cream, cream cheese, and vanilla in a bowl and mix well. Divide the cherries between the 4 ramekins. Spoon the cream mixture over the cherries, then top each serving with 1 tablespoon of the brown sugar.

Put the ramekins under the broiler until the sugar melts and begins to caramelize. Remove from the heat and serve immediately.

serves **4**

Q

V

10 oz. fresh, ripe cherries, pitted

½ cup light cream

½ cup cream cheese

1 teaspoon pure vanilla extract

¼ cup brown sugar

4 ramekins, 5 oz. each

plum clafoutis

For a very decadent dessert, use light cream instead of milk in this recipe. You can also use other stone fruits or berries.

Preheat the oven to 375°F.

Arrange the halved plums in the prepared dish. Beat the eggs in a measuring jug, add the milk, and mix well.

Sift the flour into a medium bowl, add the sugar, and make a well in the center. Slowly whisk in the milk mixture until it is all incorporated and the batter is smooth and glossy.

Pour the batter over the plums and bake in the preheated oven for about 40 minutes until golden and firm to the touch.

Lightly dust the clafoutis with confectioners' sugar just before serving.

serves **4**

V

1½ lbs. plums, halved and pitted

4 eggs

2 cups milk

½ cup all-purpose flour

½ cup sugar

confectioners' sugar, to dust

a shallow ovenproof dish, 10 inches square, lightly greased

broiled *peaches* with *pistachios* and *dates*

2 heaping tablespoons cream cheese

2 teaspoons orange juice

10 shelled pistachio nuts or other favorite nuts, roughly chopped

2 pitted dried dates, finely chopped

2 ripe peaches or nectarines

serves 2

Q

V

A delicious, easy dessert of peaches stuffed with a creamy, nutritious date and nut filling. The perfect treat for those who don't want to spend long in the kitchen.

Preheat the broiler and line the broiler pan with aluminum foil.

Meanwhile, mix together the cream cheese, orange juice, pistachios, and dates in a small bowl. Cut the peaches in half, twist to separate the fruit into halves, then prise out the pits.

Spoon the cream cheese mixture into the peach centers. Broil for 6–7 minutes until the cream cheese mixture starts to turn golden and the fruit softens.

baked amaretti *peaches* with *raspberry* sauce

3 tablespoons unsalted butter, at room temperature

3 tablespoons sugar

1 extra-large egg

½ cup ground almonds

1 oz. finely crushed amaretti cookies, about 4 small ones

6 ripe peaches

Greek yogurt, to serve

Raspberry sauce

1 cup fresh raspberries (or frozen and defrosted)

1 tablespoon confectioners' sugar

1 tablespoon lemon juice

a 12-cup muffin pan (optional)

makes 12

V

These must be eaten soon after baking, but the filling can be made in advance and chilled until needed. If you don't have a muffin pan, make rings out of foil to keep the peaches upright.

Preheat the oven to 350°F.

Put the butter and sugar in a bowl and beat until blended. Beat in the egg. Stir in the ground almonds and amaretti until well mixed. Set aside.

Cut the peaches in half, twist to separate the fruit into halves, then prise out the pits. Scrape out a bit more from each hollow to make more space for the filling. Divide the filling between the peaches. Put a peach half into each muffin cup to keep them upright while baking.

Bake in the preheated oven until the filling is puffed and golden, about 25–30 minutes. To make the raspberry sauce, mash the raspberries, confectioners' sugar, and lemon juice together in a bowl. Serve the peaches warm, with yogurt and the raspberry sauce.

*broiled peaches with
pistachios and dates*

chocolate brownies

Who doesn't love chocolate brownies? They're pretty easy to make but the skill is in the timing: it's easy to think your brownies aren't cooked and to give them those extra few minutes in the oven, which can dry them out and turn them into a mealy chocolate cake. So be brave—if the mixture doesn't wobble in the middle and a skewer inserted in the center comes out chocolatey, remove the brownies from the oven and by the time they have cooled, they will be perfect.

Preheat the oven to 350°F.

Put the chocolate pieces and butter in a heatproof bowl set over a pan of simmering water. Do not let the bottom of the bowl touch the water. Leave for several minutes until the chocolate has melted, then remove the bowl from the pan and let cool slightly.

Whisk together the eggs and the sugar with a handheld electric whisk. Pour in the melted chocolate mixture, then add the salt and finally the flour. Whisk until well blended. Pour the mixture into the prepared pan and bake in the center of the preheated oven for 23–25 minutes (you have to be precise with brownies!) The outside should look crackled and the inside will feel firm to the touch but will be gooey underneath. Remove from the oven and let cool in the pan for 15 minutes, then slice into squares or bars.

To make the vanilla cream, take a small, sharp knife and run it carefully down the length of the vanilla bean. Open out the bean and scrape out the tiny black seeds with the tip of the knife. Stir the vanilla seeds into the crème fraîche or whipped cream and serve with a brownie square or two.

8 oz. bittersweet chocolate, broken into pieces

2 sticks unsalted butter, at room temperature

4 extra-large eggs, beaten

1¾ cups sugar

½ teaspoon salt

1 cup self-rising flour

2 tablespoons cocoa powder

Vanilla cream

¾ cup crème fraîche or very lightly whipped heavy cream

1 vanilla bean

a baking pan, 8 x 12 inches, greased and lined with parchment paper

chocolate and *cinnamon* brownies

½ cup shelled hazelnuts

10 oz. bittersweet chocolate, broken into pieces

2 sticks unsalted butter

3 eggs

1 cup plus 2 tablespoons sugar

½ cup self-rising flour

2 teaspoons ground cinnamon

⅔ cup white chocolate chips

a baking pan, 9 x 13 inches, greased and lined with parchment paper

These are sophisticated brownies, made with bittersweet and white chocolate, so the better the chocolate, the better they will taste. Most people can't resist eating them the minute they come out of the oven. Perfect with a cup of coffee.

Preheat the oven to 375°F.

Put the hazelnuts into a dry skillet and toast over medium heat until aromatic. They burn quickly so keep an eye on them and shake the skillet regularly. Let them cool, then chop coarsely.

Put the chocolate pieces and butter in a heatproof bowl set over a pan of simmering water. Do not let the bottom of the bowl touch the water. Leave for several minutes until the chocolate has melted, then remove the bowl from the pan and let cool slightly. Put the eggs and sugar into another bowl and beat until pale. Stir in the melted chocolate, flour, cinnamon, white chocolate chips, and hazelnuts. Pour the mixture into the prepared pan and bake in the preheated oven for 35–40 minutes until the top sets but the mixture still feels soft underneath. Remove from the oven and let cool in the pan for 15 minutes, then slice into squares.

peanut butter brownies

Chocolate and peanuts are a classic combination. Use peanut butter with no added sugar or fat as it gives the best flavor.

Preheat the oven to 350°F.

Put the chocolate pieces and butter in a heatproof bowl set over a pan of simmering water. Do not let the bottom of the bowl touch the water. Leave for several minutes until the chocolate has melted, then remove the bowl from the pan and let cool slightly. Break the eggs into another bowl and beat well with a handheld electric whisk. Add the sugar and whisk until the mixture is very thick and mousse-like. Whisk in the melted chocolate. Sift the flour and cocoa onto the mixture and mix until well combined. Spoon the mixture into the prepared pan.

Put all the ingredients for the peanut mixture into a bowl and mix well. Drop teaspoonfuls of the mixture, evenly spaced, onto the chocolate mixture. Use a teaspoon handle to marble or swirl both mixtures. Scatter the peanuts over the top. Bake in the preheated oven for about 30 minutes or until just firm. Remove from the oven and let cool in the pan for 15 minutes, then slice into squares or bars.

makes
16

V

3½ oz. bittersweet chocolate, broken into pieces

1½ sticks unsalted butter, diced

3 extra-large eggs

1¼ cups brown sugar

1 scant cup all-purpose flour

2 tablespoons cocoa powder

Peanut mixture

¾ cup smooth peanut butter

¼ cup sugar

1 tablespoon all-purpose flour

¼ cup milk

2 tablespoons roasted, unsalted peanuts

a baking pan, 8 x 10 inches, greased and lined with parchment paper

mint brownies

4½ oz. bittersweet chocolate, broken into pieces

7 tablespoons unsalted butter, diced

3 extra-large eggs

1 cup sugar

¾ cup all-purpose flour

2 tablespoons cocoa powder

4–7 oz. bittersweet chocolate with mint center (depending on strength of flavor required)

a baking pan, 8 x 10 inches, greased and lined with parchment paper

For this unusual brownie recipe you'll need a box (or bar) of bittersweet chocolate with a soft, mint-flavored fondant center, of the type that is most often sold as "after-dinner" mints. The mints turn these brownies into a dessert fit for fine dining with friends.

Preheat the oven to 350°F.

Put the chocolate and butter in a heatproof bowl set over a pan of simmering water. Do not let the bottom of the bowl touch the water. Leave for several minutes until the chocolate has melted, then remove the bowl from the pan and let cool slightly.

Whisk the eggs with a handheld electric whisk, then add the sugar and beat until thick and mousse-like. Whisk in the melted chocolate. Sift the flour and cocoa onto the mixture and stir in. When thoroughly combined spoon half the brownie mixture into the prepared pan and spread evenly.

Leave the mint chocolates whole or break them up (depending on the size of the ones you are using). Arrange them over the brownie mixture already in the pan. Spoon the remaining brownie mixture on top and gently spread to cover the chocolate mints.

Bake in the preheated oven for about 25 minutes or until a skewer inserted halfway between the sides and the center comes out just clean (though some of the sticky mint layer will appear). Remove from the oven and let cool in the pan for 15 minutes, then slice into squares or bars.

english *flapjacks*

These chewy oat bars taste so good that it's hard to believe they are a healthy and sustaining snack to keep you going for hours.

makes
8

V

Preheat the oven to 300°F.

Melt the butter in a large saucepan, add the syrup and sugar, and stir until the sugar has dissolved. Remove from the heat and stir in the oats. Spoon the mixture into the prepared baking pan and bake in the preheated oven for 20 minutes. When done, cut into squares straightaway and let cool.

13 tablespoons unsalted butter

1 tablespoon maple syrup

1 scant cup brown sugar

2 cups rolled oats

a shallow baking pan, 8 x 12 inches, lined with parchment paper

honeyjacks

Flapjacks with a twist—the same chewy, sweet taste, but with the extra flavors of honey, shredded coconut, and raisins.

makes
8

V

Preheat the oven to 300°F.

Melt the butter in a large saucepan, add the syrup, sugar, and honey, then stir until the sugar has dissolved. Remove from the heat and stir in the oats and raisins. Spoon the mixture into the prepared baking pan, sprinkle with the coconut, and bake in the preheated oven for 20 minutes. When done, cut into squares straightaway and let cool before eating.

13 tablespoons unsalted butter

1 tablespoon maple syrup

⅓ cup brown sugar

⅓ cup honey

2 cups rolled oats

⅓ cup raisins

1 cup shredded coconut

a shallow baking pan, 8 x 12 inches, lined with parchment paper

nutty jacks

Nuts are high in protein and fiber, so they make a healthy addition to flapjacks. Use whichever type of nuts you like.

makes
8

V

Preheat the oven to 300°F.

Melt the butter in a large saucepan, add the syrup and sugar, and stir until the sugar has dissolved. Remove from the heat and stir in the oats and nuts. Spoon the mixture into the prepared baking pan and bake in the preheated oven for 20 minutes. When done, cut into squares straightaway and let cool. Drizzle the melted chocolate over the nutty jacks in a zigzag pattern and let set before eating.

13 tablespoons unsalted butter

1 tablespoon maple syrup

1 scant cup brown sugar

2 cups rolled oats

⅓ cup chopped nuts

4–6 oz. bittersweet chocolate, melted

a shallow baking pan, 8 x 12 inches, lined with parchment paper

nutty *plum* crumble

serves 4

V

12 plums, halved and pitted

2–3 thick strips of zest and the juice from 1 unwaxed orange

⅓ cup brown sugar

1 stick unsalted butter, chilled and diced

¾ cup self-rising flour

⅓ cup ground almonds

3 tablespoons slivered almonds

3 tablespoons pine nuts

cream, to serve (optional)

an ovenproof dish

Pine nuts and almonds with their toasty flavors add another dimension to this crumble. They make for a crunchy, tasty crust which needs to settle before it crisps up, so leave the crumble to cool down slightly and eat it when it's warm rather than piping hot. Serve with cream if you want to make it super indulgent. Some of the other winning fruit combinations you could try are apple and blackberry, apple and pear, or mango and banana.

Preheat the oven to 350°F.

Put the plums in the ovenproof dish—there should be enough room left to accommodate the topping. Add the orange zest and juice. Sprinkle over 2 tablespoons of the sugar and dot over 2 tablespoons of the butter. Cover with aluminum foil and bake in the preheated oven for 25–30 minutes, or until the plums are beginning to soften.

Put the flour, ground almonds, and the remaining butter in a bowl and rub until it forms small lumps. Stir in the slivered almonds, pine nuts, and the remaining sugar.

Remove the dish from the oven, discard the foil, and scatter over the crumble topping. Bake for 30 minutes, or until the topping is golden and the juices are bubbling through. Remove from the oven and let stand for 10 minutes to allow the crust to firm up. Transfer to bowls and serve with cream, if you like.

nectarine and *ginger* crumble

This is a useful recipe for when nectarines are slightly hard, as cooking them softens the flesh and brings out the flavor. Ginger goes particularly well with this fruit so ginger cookies have been used here but if they are not available, simply substitute them with any favorite crunchy cookie and add a good pinch or two of ground ginger to the topping mixture.

serves
4

V

6 nectarines (or a mixture of peaches and plums)

2 tablespoons finely chopped fresh ginger

¼ cup apple juice

¼ cup sugar

vanilla ice cream, to serve

Ginger topping

1 stick unsalted butter, melted

7 oz. gingersnap cookies, crushed

½ cup light brown sugar

a baking sheet

a shallow ovenproof dish

Preheat the oven to 375°F and place the baking sheet on the middle shelf to heat.

Cut the nectarines in half, twist to separate the fruit into halves, then prise out the pits. Slice or chop the flesh, tip it into the ovenproof dish, and mix with the apple juice, chopped ginger, and sugar.

To make the ginger topping, melt the butter in a saucepan and stir in the crushed gingersnap cookies and sugar until the mixture resembles rough bread crumbs. (At this stage you can pop it into a plastic bag and chill in the fridge until needed.)

Lightly sprinkle the topping mixture evenly over the surface of the nectarines, mounding it up a little towards the center.

Place the ovenproof dish on top of the baking sheet in the preheated oven and bake for about 25 minutes, until crisp and golden on top. Remove from the oven and let cool for 5 minutes before serving with vanilla ice cream.

1 lb. rhubarb, chopped

2 inches fresh ginger, peeled and finely grated

2 tablespoons sugar

7 bananas, peeled and thickly cut diagonally

¼ teaspoon ground cinnamon

heavy cream, to serve

Oat topping

¾ cup all-purpose flour

6 tablespoons unsalted butter, chilled and diced

⅓ cup brown sugar

⅔ cup rolled oats

an ovenproof dish

rhubarb, ginger, and banana crumble

This version of the classic rhubarb crumble is given a banana twist, which makes a wicked combination with the ginger and crunchy oats in the crumble topping. Serve with a dollop of thick cream for a winning dessert.

Preheat the oven to 400°F.

Put the rhubarb in a medium saucepan and add the ginger, sugar, and 2 tablespoons water. Bring to a boil and simmer for 7–10 minutes, until the rhubarb has softened. Mash with a fork until you get a rough purée. Transfer to the ovenproof dish and top with the bananas and a sprinkling of cinnamon.

Put the flour and butter in a bowl and, using your fingertips, rub the butter into the flour until it looks like bread crumbs. Add the sugar and two-thirds of the oats. Sprinkle over the fruit mixture and top with the remaining oats. Bake in the preheated oven for 30–40 minutes. Serve hot with cream.

7 tablespoons butter

½ cup sugar

½ cup milk

2 eggs

1 teaspoon pure vanilla extract

1 cup self-rising flour

½ cup cocoa powder

Chocolate swamp

¾ cup brown sugar

¼ cup cocoa powder

1 cup boiling water

a 1-quart capacity ovenproof dish, greased

chocolate swamp pudding

Melt-in-the-mouth chocolate cake floating in a rich chocolate sauce—this is a sweet treat to die for.

Preheat the oven to 350°F.

Put the butter, sugar, and milk in a saucepan and heat gently until the sugar has dissolved. Set aside to cool.

Whisk the eggs in a bowl and add the vanilla. Sift the flour and cocoa into a large bowl, add the milk and the egg mixture, and stir until smooth. Pour into the prepared dish and set aside.

To make the chocolate swamp, mix the sugar and cocoa powder together, then sprinkle evenly over the top of the pudding. Pour on the boiling water and bake in the preheated oven for 25 minutes.

*rhubarb, ginger, and
banana crumble*

free-form caramelized peach tart

free-form *caramelized peach* tart

This is such a simple recipe—buy the pastry ready-made (choose an all-butter one for the most indulgent flavor) and shape it into a rustic-looking tart. You don't even need a tart pan!

Preheat the oven to 450°F.

Roll out the pastry on a lightly floured work surface and cut out a circle, 11 inches in diameter, using the plate as a template. Lift onto the baking sheet and make an edge by twisting the pastry over all the way around the edge. Press to seal. Still on the baking sheet, chill or freeze for 15 minutes.

Peel the peaches if necessary, then cut them in half, twist to separate the fruit into halves, and prise out the pits. Cut the flesh into slices. Put the butter into a saucepan, then add the lemon juice and half the sugar. Heat until melted, then add the peaches and toss gently. Pile the peaches all over the pastry. Sprinkle with the remaining sugar and bake in the preheated oven for 20–25 minutes until golden, puffed, and caramelized.

serves
6

V

1 lb. storebought puff pastry

4–6 ripe peaches or nectarines

5 tablespoons unsalted butter

juice of ½ a lemon

1 cup sugar

a dinner plate, 11 inches in diameter (to use as a template)

a baking sheet

quick french *apple* tart

To make this tart sensational and fit for a special occasion, make sure the apples are sliced as finely as possible and that they are arranged neatly and elegantly.

Preheat the oven to 400°F.

Roll out the pastry to a rectangle measuring 12 x 7 inches. Place on the baking sheet and brush all over with the egg.

Cut the apples into quarters, then slice thinly and arrange in rows on top of the pastry, leaving a 2-inch gap around the edges. Drizzle the melted butter over the apples, sprinkle with sugar, and dust with cinnamon. Brush the edges of the pastry with the remaining egg, then fold the edges inwards and gently press down.

Bake the tart in the preheated oven for 30 minutes. Reduce the heat to 350°F and bake for another 15 minutes until the tart is golden. Serve hot or at room temperature.

serves
4

V

8 oz. storebought puff pastry

1 egg, beaten with a fork

4 red apples, cored

2 tablespoons butter, melted

2 tablespoons brown sugar

½ teaspoon ground cinnamon

a baking sheet, lightly greased

lemon cornmeal cake

2 sticks unsalted butter, diced

1¼ cups sugar

4 eggs

3 unwaxed lemons

¾ cup cornmeal

¾ cup self-rising flour

light cream, to serve

an ovenproof dish, 8 inches in diameter, lightly greased

Italian cornmeal is mostly used in savory dishes, but works well in cakes to give them a coarse texture.

Preheat the oven to 350°F.

Put the butter into a mixing bowl, add the sugar, and beat until creamy and smooth. Beat in the eggs one at a time.

Grate the zest and squeeze the juice from 2½ of the lemons. Slice the remaining lemon half and set aside. Add the lemon zest and juice to the cake mixture and mix well. Add the cornmeal and flour, fold in until evenly blended, then spoon into the prepared dish. Arrange the reserved lemon slices around the middle of the cake. Bake in the preheated oven for 25 minutes. Reduce the heat to 325°F and cook for 10 minutes, until a knife inserted in the center comes out clean. Serve with cream.

devil's food cake

6 tablespoons unsalted butter

½ cup light brown sugar

⅓ cup corn syrup

1 cup all-purpose flour

¼ cup cocoa powder

1 egg, beaten

1 teaspoon baking soda

½ cup milk

Frosting

3 tablespoons cocoa powder

3 tablespoons hot water

6 tablespoons butter, softened

1¼ cups confectioners' sugar

1 tablespoon corn syrup

2 drops of pure vanilla extract

2 cake pans, 8 inches in diameter, greased

Wickedly rich and chocolatey, this cake will have everyone clamoring for more.

Preheat the oven to 350°F.

Put the butter, sugar, and syrup in a saucepan and heat gently until the sugar has dissolved.

Sift the flour and cocoa into a bowl, add the butter mixture, and stir well. Add the egg and mix again. Combine the baking soda with the milk, add to the bowl, and mix thoroughly. Divide the mixture between the prepared cake pans and smooth out with a spatula. Bake in the preheated oven for 20 minutes, until just firm to the touch. Turn out onto a wire rack to cool.

To make the frosting, put the cocoa in a bowl and mix in the hot water. Add the butter, sugar, syrup, and vanilla and beat until smooth.

When the cakes are cold, sandwich together with some of the frosting. Dip a spatula in hot water to prevent the frosting sticking to it. Spread the remainder of the frosting over the top and sides of the cake.

lemon cornmeal cake

carrot cake

A scrumptious teatime treat—no wonder it's also known as "passion cake!"

Preheat the oven to 350°F.

Put the egg yolks and sugar in a bowl and whisk until thick and creamy. Add all the remaining ingredients, except the egg white, and fold carefully until the mixture is smooth.

Whisk the egg whites until stiff, then fold into the cake mixture. Pour into the prepared pan and bake in the center of the preheated oven for 1 hour. When done, let the cake cool in the pan for 5 minutes, then turn out and let cool completely on a wire rack.

To make the frosting, beat the cheese and confectioners' sugar together with a wooden spoon until light and fluffy. Add a little orange zest and juice to flavor. Spread over the top of the cold cake using a spatula dipped in hot water. Sprinkle with the remaining orange zest.

4 eggs, separated

1 cup brown sugar

zest and juice of 1 orange

1⅓ cups ground walnuts

1 teaspoon ground cinnamon

1½ cups grated carrots

¾ cup whole-wheat flour

1 teaspoon baking powder

Frosting

1 cup cream cheese

⅔ cup confectioners' sugar

finely grated zest and juice of 1 small orange

a loose-bottomed cake pan, 8 inches square, greased

---

banana cake

This cake is popular even with those who don't like bananas. The flavor improves with keeping, so wrap the cake in plastic wrap and keep for a couple of days before cutting.

Preheat the oven to 350°F.

Put the sugar and syrup in a bowl. Put the oil, eggs, bananas, and vanilla in another bowl and whizz with a handheld electric whisk. Add to the bowl of sugar and mix until smooth. Fold in the flour and baking powder, then spoon into the prepared pan. Bake in the middle of the preheated oven for 50–60 minutes. When it is done, a skewer inserted in the center of the cake should come out clean.

¾ cup sugar

1 tablespoon corn syrup

¾ cup vegetable oil

2 eggs

2 ripe bananas, peeled and mashed

1 teaspoon pure vanilla extract

2¼ cups self-rising flour

1 teaspoon baking powder

a 9 x 5-inch loaf pan, lightly greased

lemon drizzle loaf

serves
6–8

V

1½ sticks unsalted butter, softened

1¾ cups sugar

3 extra-large eggs, at room temperature

1¾ cups self-rising flour

½ teaspoon baking powder

2 unwaxed lemons

½ cup milk, at room temperature

a large loaf pan, about 16 x 5 x 4 inches, greased and lined with parchment paper

Unwaxed lemons are best if you can find them, because you need both the skin and juice for this simple but tangy loaf cake.

Preheat the oven to 350°F.

Put the butter, 1¼ cups of the sugar, and the eggs in a large bowl. Sift in the flour and baking powder. Grate the zest from the lemons straight into the bowl, then reserve the lemons.

Add the milk, then beat with a wooden spoon or handheld electric whisk (on low speed) for 1 minute until smooth and well mixed, with no streaks of flour.

Spoon the mixture into the prepared pan and bake in the preheated oven for 50–55 minutes. A skewer inserted in the center should come out clean. If it is sticky with mixture, then bake the loaf for another 5 minutes.

While the loaf is cooking, make the drizzle. Squeeze the juice from the reserved lemons into a small bowl. Add the remaining sugar and stir for 1 minute until the sugar has dissolved and you have a syrupy glaze.

When the loaf is cooked, remove it from the oven and stand the pan on a wire rack. Prick the top of the loaf all over with a toothpick to make small holes. Spoon the lemon syrup all over the top so it trickles into the holes. Leave until completely cold before lifting the cake out of the pan. Peel off the parchment paper and cut the loaf into thick slices.

apple cake

apple cake

This looks every bit as delicious as it tastes. It makes a scrumptious dessert with some ice cream, but is also good for tucking into a lunchbox or picnic hamper.

Preheat the oven to 300°F.

Beat the butter and sugar together in a large bowl with a handheld electric whisk until smooth, light, and fluffy. Add the eggs, a little at a time, stirring well between each addition. Stir in the almonds, flour, baking powder, and lemon zest, and finally the milk. Spoon the mixture into the loaf pan.

Cut the apples into thin slices. Arrange evenly over the cake. Bake in the preheated oven for 45 minutes or so, until the cake has risen and is golden and springy to the touch. Remove the cake from the oven and let cool in the pan for 20 minutes, then turn out onto a wire rack to cool completely. Dust with confectioners' sugar.

serves
6–8

V

1 stick plus 2 tablespoons unsalted butter

¾ cup sugar

2 eggs, lightly beaten with a fork

1 cup ground almonds

scant ½ cup all-purpose flour

1 teaspoon baking powder

grated zest of 1 unwaxed lemon

⅓ cup milk

2 red apples, cored

confectioners' sugar, to dust

a 9 x 5-inch loaf pan, greased and just the base lined with parchment paper

basic cake

This light, moist yellow cake can be dressed up or down to suit any occasion. Use it as a base for your favorite flavorings.

Preheat the oven to 350°F.

Put the margarine and sugar in a bowl and beat with a wooden spoon until light and fluffy. Beat in the eggs, then stir in the vanilla. Sift in the flour and baking powder, then fold together quickly with a large spoon (speed at this stage keeps the cake light). Spoon the mixture into the prepared pan and bake in the middle of the preheated oven for 30–35 minutes. When done, a skewer inserted in the center of the cake should come out clean; if it doesn't, cook for a further 5–10 minutes. Let cool in the pan for 5 minutes, then turn out onto a wire rack and let cool completely.

To make the frosting, sift the sugar into a bowl and stir in the lemon juice. Carefully add a little water to make a smooth, stiff paste. Use a wet spatula to spread the frosting over the top. Let set before serving.

serves
6–8

V

20 tablespoons margarine

1½ cups sugar

5 eggs

1 teaspoon pure vanilla extract

2¾ cups self-rising flour

1 teaspoon baking powder

Frosting

1½ cups confectioners' sugar

juice of 1 lemon

a shallow baking pan, 8 x 12 inches, lined with parchment paper

chocolate chocolate chip cake

3½ oz. bittersweet chocolate, broken into pieces

7 tablespoons unsalted butter

1 cup sugar

1 cup cream cheese (not low-fat)

2 eggs

1½ cups all-purpose flour

1½ teaspoons baking powder

a pinch of salt

3½ oz. chocolate chips

a loaf pan, 9 x 5 x 3 inches, greased and lined with parchment paper

serves
6–8

V

This is a basic chocolate cake but you can either keep it simple, as in the recipe below, or add a few unbeatable additions. Try a good handful or so of mini marshmallows thrown in with the chocolate chips. Coarsely chopped almonds or hazelnuts are good as well, or instead of. If you were to add a heaping teaspoon of ground cinnamon, it would have a distinctly Mexican flavor. Despite the cream cheese, a generous dollop of something else creamy makes it even better.

Preheat the oven to 375°F.

Put the chocolate and butter in a heatproof bowl set over a pan of simmering water. Do not let the bottom of the bowl touch the water. Leave for several minutes until the chocolate has melted, then remove the bowl from the pan and let cool slightly.

Put the sugar and cream cheese in a mixing bowl and beat with a handheld electric whisk (on high speed) until well blended. Add the eggs and melted chocolate and continue beating until well mixed.

Put the flour, baking powder, and salt in another bowl and mix well. Add to the cream cheese mixture, with the whisk on low speed, until just blended. Fold in the chocolate chips. Pour into the prepared pan and bake in the preheated oven for about 40–45 minutes. A skewer inserted in the center should come out clean.

index

conversion charts

Weights and measures have been rounded up or down slightly to make measuring easier.

A US stick of butter weighs 4 oz. which is approximately 115 g or 8 tablespoons.

Volume equivalents

American	Metric	Imperial
1 teaspoon	5 ml	
1 tablespoon	15 ml	
¼ cup	60 ml	2 fl.oz.
⅓ cup	75 ml	2½ fl.oz.
½ cup	125 ml	4 fl.oz.
⅔ cup	150 ml	5 fl.oz. (¼ pint)
¾ cup	175 ml	6 fl.oz.
1 cup	250 ml	8 fl.oz.

Weight equivalents

Imperial	Metric
1 oz.	25 g
2 oz.	50 g
3 oz.	75 g
4 oz.	125 g
5 oz.	150 g
6 oz.	175 g
7 oz.	200 g
8 oz. (½ lb.)	250 g
9 oz.	275 g
10 oz.	300 g
11 oz.	325 g
12 oz.	375 g
13 oz.	400 g
14 oz.	425 g
15 oz.	475 g
16 oz. (1 lb.)	500 g
2 lbs.	1 kg

Measurements

Inches	cm
¼ inch	5 mm
½ inch	1 cm
¾ inch	1.5 cm
1 inch	2.5 cm
2 inches	5 cm
3 inches	7 cm
4 inches	10 cm
5 inches	12 cm
6 inches	15 cm
7 inches	18 cm
8 inches	20 cm
9 inches	23 cm
10 inches	25 cm
11 inches	28 cm
12 inches	30 cm

Oven temperatures

250°F	120°C	Gas ½
275°F	140°C	Gas 1
300°F	150°C	Gas 2
325°F	160°C	Gas 3
350°F	180°C	Gas 4
375°F	190°C	Gas 5
400°F	200°C	Gas 6
425°F	220°C	Gas 7
450°F	230°C	Gas 8
475°F	240°C	Gas 9

recipe credits

Nadia Arumugam
Indonesian fried rice
Sweet and sour pork

Susannah Blake
Giant prosciutto, brie, and tomato toasts
Mushrooms on toast
Nutty chocolate and marshmallow toast
Spicy fried potatoes and chorizo on toast
Tomato, basil, and mozzarella toasts
Tuna melt

Tamsin Burnett-Hall
Bean burritos
Chickpea and vegetable bulgur pilau
Moussaka-filled eggplant
Tarragon chicken casserole

Maxine Clark
Bell peppers stuffed with pasta
Broiled portobello mushrooms
Butternut squash, sage, and chile risotto
Creamy tomato and bread soup
Free-form caramelized peach tart
Muffin mania
Nectarine and ginger crumble
Parmesan and butter risotto
Quiche Lorraine
Sausage and bacon rolls
Sausage, sun-dried tomato, and potato tart

Linda Collister
Bang bang chicken
Beef rendang
Cinnamon toast
Double chocolate muffins
Guacamole
Home-baked tortilla chips
Italian roast chicken
Lemon drizzle loaf
Mint brownies
Pea and Parmesan risotto
Peanut butter brownies
Pigs-in-a-blanket
Roasties

Ross Dobson
Asparagus tagliatelle
Baked pasta with eggplant...
Chunky chickpea soup
Garlic and chile rice soup
Miso soup with ramen noodles
Scotch broth
Sesame chicken and vegetable noodle salad
Zucchini and tomato risotto

Silvana Franco
Creamy smoked salmon pasta
English breakfast pizza
Lasagne
Margherita pizza
Pasta and bean soup
Pasta with prosciutto...
Pasta with puttanesca sauce
Pasta with roasted eggplant...
Penne with broccoli...
Pepperoni pizza
Quattro stagioni pizza
Roasted bell pepper pizza
Soup with pasta shells, peas...
Spaghetti Bolognese
Summer minestrone
Three-cheese baked penne
White spaghetti

Liz Franklin
Apple cake
Cannellini beans with garlic...
Lemony poached chicken
Little fried mozzarella and tomato sandwiches
Meatloaf
Pea, sausage, and onion calzone
Rosemary potatoes
Super-easy lamb skewers

Tonia George
Chicken avgolemono
Chickpea, tomato, and chorizo soup
Chocolate brownies
Corn and pancetta chowder
Couscous with feta, dill...
Cumin-spiced lamb chops
Minty pea risotto soup
Nutty plum crumble
Puy lentil and vegetable soup
Rigatoni with pork...
Split pea and sausage soup
Steak with new potatoes, Roquefort, and arugula
Zucchini, fava bean, and lemon broth

Brian Glover
Fish baked with lemon, oregano, and potatoes

Nicola Graimes
Broiled peaches
Bubble and squeak patties
Mozzarella and tuna quesadilla
Pesto and mozzarella toastie
Sardines and tomato on toast
Vegetable, ham, and barley broth
Turkey and bay skewers
Pork with sweet potato mash
Rigatoni with bacon...

Rachael Anne Hill
Baked sweet potatoes
Broccoli cheese
Cheat's cherry brûlée
Cheat's mini pizzas
Flaked haddock moussaka
Foil-baked salmon
Leeks and tomatoes on toast
Tuna pasta salad
Tuscan tuna and bean pasta

Jennifer Joyce
Bacon, potato, and Red Leicester panini
Gruyère, sharp Cheddar, and scallion panini

Caroline Marson
Beef fajitas
Moroccan-style roasted vegetable couscous
Pepperoni, bell pepper, and crouton frittata
Roast chicken with garlic...
Stir-fried seafood

Jane Noraika
Rhubarb, ginger, and banana crumble
Roasted vegetable dauphinois
Sesame sweet potato wedges

Elsa Petersen-Schepelern
Minestrone

Louise Pickford
Cheese on toast
Cherry tomato puttanesca sauce
Chicken lemon skewers
Chocolate and cinnamon brownies
Fusilli with sausage ragu
Greek country salad
Lamb in pita bread
Roasted tomato sauce
Shrimp fried rice
Sour cream coleslaw
Stir-fried sesame cabbage
Tomato, caper, and anchovy pizza

Jennie Shapter
Baked brunch omelet
Chile chicken enchiladas
Minted zucchini frittata
Onion and blue cheese omelet
Spaghetti and arugula frittata

Fiona Smith
Garlic and tomato naan
Greek barley salad
New potato, crisp salami, and sesame salad
Roast potatoes, chorizo, and lemon
Tzatziki

Sunil Vijayakar
Chicken and spinach curry
Ground beef and pea curry
Spiced eggplant dhal

Fran Warde
Banana cake
Basic cake
Carrot cake
Chocolate swamp pudding
Creamy mustard mash
Devil's food cake
English flapjacks
Farmhouse sauté
Fish cakes
French pancakes
French toast and fried tomatoes
Garlic and parsley bread
Hamburgers
Honeyjacks
Indian lamb curry
Lemon cornmeal cake
Noodle mountain
Nutty jacks
Plum clafoutis
Potato skins with green dip
Potatoes boulangère
Prosciutto-wrapped salmon
Quick French apple tart
Ratatouille
Rice noodle salad with shrimp
Risotto primavera
Scrambled eggs
Shrimp curry
Spicy vegetable wrap
Thai green chicken curry
Three-cheese cauliflower
Toasted oat yogurt
Vegetable noodle stir-fry
Vegetable, seed, and nut cakes

Laura Washburn
Baked amaretti peaches
Chicken with tomato, garlic...
Chocolate chocolate chip cake
Kitchen garden soup
Pasta with ricotta...
Potato wedges
Vodka risotto

Lindy Wildsmith
Carbonara
Spaghetti with garlic...
Tuna, coriander, and lemon pasta with tomato salad

photography credits

Key: a=above, b=below, r=right, l=left, c=center.

Caroline Arber
Pages 17a, 36r, 37, 52, 75, 76, 96, 185, 197a, 201, 216, 228

Martin Brigdale
Pages 55, 107b, 112, 131, 132, 149a, 149c, 172, 175, 189, 224

Peter Cassidy
Pages 3 all, 6, 8, 11 all, 12bl, 12-13b, 13a, 13b, 23l, 57a, 57b, 80, 84, 87, 91, 92, 106, 107c, 115, 127, 136, 182, 190, 212, 220

Vanessa Davies
Pages 18, 99, 103l, 107a, 128, 178r, 186, 194, 205, 231

Nicki Dowey
Pages 4-5, 28, 95, 121l, 159r, 206

Dan Duchars
Page 196

Tara Fisher
Pages 17c, 38, 144, 164, 168

Lisa Linder
Pages 31, 47, 103r, 232

William Lingwood
Pages 23r, 24, 27, 36l, 44, 66, 69, 79, 88, 108, 121r, 122, 147,
154, 159l, 193, 198, 223

Richard Jung
Pages 58, 61, 119, 149b, 150, 153, 160, 167, 171, 197c, 213, 215

Diana Miller
Pages 21, 100, 140

David Munns
Pages 14ar, 17b, 43r, 125l, 163, 235

Noel Murphy
Pages 41, 43l, 51, 70r, 202

William Reavell
Pages 32, 35 both, 57c, 62, 72, 83, 104, 111, 116, 135, 139, 143, 157, 176, 181, 197b, 209, 210, 219

Yuki Sugiura
Page 65

Debi Treloar
Pages 2, 12-13a, 14al, 14bl, 15, 16, 48, 56, 148, 227

Ian Wallace
Pages 1, 70l, 125r

Kate Whitaker
Page 178l